Our Awesome God is a user-friendly approach to the
character and nature of God. Each chapter reviews the
biblical doctrine of a particular attribute, its application,
and an appropriate response.

To Grace

To seek the Lord – this is the greatest need
To find the Lord – this is the greatest discovery
To know the Lord – this is the greatest joy
To love the Lord – this is the greatest wisdom
To serve the Lord – this is the greatest accomplishment

Our Awesome God

Ken M. Campbell

Christian Focus

Acknowledgments

In writing this book, I have received welcome comments and suggestions from Nancy Whetstone, Corinne Livesay, Rob Waltzer, Wynn Kenyon and Arthur Holmes. I am especially thankful for the editorial skills and the many helpful suggestions offered by David Murray. To them all I owe a debt of gratitude; the errors and inadequacies that remain are of course mine alone.

Contents

Foreword 7

Introduction 9

1. Who Made God? – the attribute of aseity 13

2. Why is there not Nothing? – the attribute of creativity 25

3. Royal Freedom – the attribute of sovereignty 37

4. The Rock – the attribute of immutability 49

5. Awesomely Different – the attribute of holiness 61

6. Comprehensive Knowledge – the attribute of omniscience 73

7. The 'How-To' God – the attribute of wisdom 83

8. The Righteous Judge – the attribute of righteousness 95

9. How Good is God? – the attribute of goodness 107

10. Settled Hostility – the attribute of wrath 121

11. Perfect Love – the attribute of love 133

12. Total Consistency – the attribute of faithfulness 147

Foreword

If you had slipped into the small Hosie Room of the University of Aberdeen Students' Union around eight o'clock on almost any Friday night in 1965-1967 you would almost certainly have found both Ken Campbell and myself gathering with around sixty to a hundred other students. We were enthusiastic members of the University Evangelical Union, proudly, if somewhat tenuously, tracing our lineage back to the gatherings the remarkable young Henry Scougal (1650-1678) organised with his even younger students.

The scene in the Hosie Room might today seem to belong to a different era. A brief welcome and introduction, an opening prayer, and then an exposition of Scripture which would last anywhere between forty minutes and (the record in my day) an hour and a half. Here I remember listening to John Stott and Eric Alexander, to William Still and James and George Philip. In these years too we heard Professor R. A. Finlayson and Professor John Murray. Others, perhaps less known but greatly gifted came to speak and invest precious time and energy in our young lives. A closing prayer would be followed by eager conversation or a browse at the book table (laden with such legends as T. C. Hammond, Francis Schaeffer, and yes, Calvin, Bunyan, Owen and many others). Then back to our residences aglow with the things we were learning and the joys of knowing and serving Christ.

To those days, to those who came to teach us, to our friends from that formative period of our lives – now spread across not only Scotland but the world serving Christ – I suspect Ken Campbell and others like myself owe more than we could ever say. These were great days in our Christian lives when our first desires to serve Christ with our whole lives were taking shape.

Since then Ken Campbell has travelled far and assembled impressive credentials in academic theology: a B.D. and Th.M. from Westminster Theological Seminary, followed by a Ph.D. from the University of Manchester. He has broad experience in teaching and pastoral ministry and now serves as a Professor in the Bible Department of Belhaven College, a well-known Presbyterian College in Jackson, Mississippi.

All of this well-qualifies him to write these pages. But I, for one, am especially delighted to see in them something more than many years of study. Here you will also find honest Christian experience and, I detect, in addition, the desire to continue the splendid tradition of which we have been beneficiaries. For Ken Campbell not only takes the truths of Scripture and explains and applies them in order to clarify our thinking about God; he does this with a view to these truths becoming faith-producing, wisdom-increasing, life-changing and character-forming. The best thing of all is that this book may help you to get to know God better. I pray it will.

Sinclair B. Ferguson
Westminster Theological Seminary
Philadelphia, Pennsylvania, USA

INTRODUCTION

Most of us can remember where we were when Neil Armstrong first set foot on the moon in July of 1969. His words – 'That's one small step for man, one giant leap for mankind' – are considered the most famous broadcast ever. Whatever we were doing, wherever we were at the time, we stopped for at least a moment to contemplate an amazing feat of engineering and planning. Somebody, somewhere, said, 'This is awesome!'

Some years later, we saw a real life-and-death drama unfold on our television screens when an airliner crashed into the Potomac River, leaving survivors struggling to stay afloat in the icy river. The freezing water had already claimed several lives, when an on-looker dived in to battle his way to a drowning woman. When he had rescued her and, incredibly, managed to drag her to shore and safety, dozens of people on the riverbank and millions more at home cheered one man's courage. Someone, somewhere, cried out, 'What an awesome achievement!'

In 1991 the United States and its allies employed their most advanced weapons systems and technologies in the Persian Gulf War. Modern communications allowed us to witness the devastation of Operation Desert Storm, often live and in full color. Over and over commentators, who had reported from conflicts all over the world, described these results as 'Awesome!'

When the Buffalo Bills trailed 34-3 in a professional football league championship game, and back-up quarterback

Frank Reich came off the bench and out of obscurity to lead his team to an overtime victory over the Houston Oilers, one hysterical commentator abandoned professional poise to call it the greatest football game ever. Fans everywhere agreed, and declared the game 'Truly awesome!'

But we also have become used to hearing advertisers portray their automobiles, soft drinks, toothpaste, or bathroom tissue as 'awesome!' Teenagers comment on each other's T-shirts and haircuts as 'awesome'. Diners describe a meal as 'awesome'. Couch potatoes assert that a movie is 'awesome'. Once upon a time, the word 'awesome' meant just that. Today it has become just another way to say what another generation used to call 'neat' or 'cool'.

It is not so long ago that 'awesome' was used to refer to God and to God alone. The dictionary still defines the term as 'full of reverential fear and wonder'. Awe is a very good word to describe the appropriate human response to the glory, the majesty, the power and the divinity of the living God. Anyone who takes a few moments to contemplate the character of this mighty, glorious Being who created us and has revealed himself in nature and Scripture is bound to employ the term awesome to describe him.

The purpose of this book is to incite the reader to a sense of awe, of reverential wonder, as you read through these pages and study the variegated character of almighty God.

Recent surveys confirm what many Christian authorities have claimed for several years: Christians have joined the 'therapeutic culture'. Instead of reading books about God and about doctrine, Christians – those who read at all, that is – study 'recovery' books, self-help books, ten-steps-to-a-more-wonderful-you books, and simple fiction. More and more believers are going to counseling sessions; more and more of their conversations are about their problems. Fewer and fewer talk about or take counsel with the Lord. But as Dr. Martyn Lloyd-Jones used to say, your real problem is *not* your 'problem' of the moment; your real problem is that *you do not know God very well*.

This book is designed to help the reader develop a better knowledge of, and relationship with, the true and living God. Not the god of personal choice, but the God who is – the awesome God. It is my prayerful hope that it will assist you in your brief pilgrimage on this earth. It is written for younger Christians in particular, and can be used in group discussions and Sunday School classes, as well as a supplement to devotional reading. May the Lord of glory draw near to you as you study and meditate on our awesome God!

Chapter One

Who Made God?

The attribute of
Aseity

I am the Alpha and the Omega who is, who was, and who is to come, the Almighty (Rev. 1:8).

A little boy: 'Mom, who made me?'

Mother: 'God made you, son.'

Boy: 'Who made the world?'

Mother: 'God made the world.'

Boy: 'Who made God?'

Mother: 'No one made God; God just is.'

Boy: 'I don't understand.'

Mother: 'Neither do I, but that's the way it is!'

Who made God?

It's a natural question coming from a child, but it is the wrong question for a child of God. Not because the answer is difficult, but because the question makes a false assumption. To ask 'Who made God?' assumes that God is part of the created universe, and that God is therefore dependent on the universe, that he can be understood by the same methods that humans and the rest of creation can be understood. Asking 'Who made God?' is the same as asking that the Creator be put under a microscope for our casual study.

But God is dependent upon nothing, because he was not created. God, and God alone, is self-existent, completely independent. There is a term for it used by theologians since Anselm in the eleventh century: *aseity*. It refers to the self-existence of God.

Centuries before Anselm, Isaiah made the point very well:

> Before him all the nations are as nothing;
>   they are regarded by him as worthless
>   and less than nothing.
> To whom, then, will you compare God?
>   What image will you compare him to? (Isa. 40:17,18).

It could not be put more clearly: we cannot compare God to anything because he is unique in nature, incomparable in his self-existence.

Yet in contrast to God the Creator who is independent, we the creation are completely dependent upon God. All attempts to be 'free' from God, to declare our independence from God, end in ruin – of which we have plentiful examples.

According to his biographer, the young Ernest Hemingway developed the 'willed determination to be a free soul, untrapped by tradition, living his life with pragmatic principles'. Having divorced himself from Christianity and what he called traditional morality (not to mention three wives along the way), he spent his life seeking adventure in Europe, Africa, Cuba and the United States. His acute observations of life, especially in times of war, certainly enabled him to produce remarkable literature. His last great book, *The Old Man and the Sea*, won the Nobel Prize that climaxed his career.

Hemingway found adventure – he was injured in Italy in the First World War, he was a correspondent in the Spanish Civil War, he was an aviator with the Royal Air Force in World War II. He also pursued his hedonistic autonomy across three continents. It produced great writing, but left him utterly disillusioned, despairing of mankind and of himself. His last novel seems to argue that dignity and value can be found by humanity in achieving some small task, done alone and done well. But, also that there is no victory, no joy, no heaven for the would-be independent man. Accordingly, one of the twentieth century's most honored authors shot himself at the age of 62.

George Eastman left a suicide note that reflected a similar idea: 'I have done all I can. Why wait?' A brilliant inventor

who became an astute businessman – a rare combination! –
Eastman developed Kodak film and the Kodak camera
which revolutionized photography worldwide. He was also a
generous philanthropist and left many monuments to his
genius and acumen. Yet at the end of it all, when he had
'done all he could', Eastman saw no point in life beyond his
own actions. So, he killed himself.

The independent person is a lonely, sad figure. The cry for
complete freedom and independence sounds very attractive
in the safe confines of a college classroom. But total self-
sufficiency looks very different in the middle of the Sahara
Desert with no support systems! Yet even if a human could
take care of his own physical needs, he would find his own
spiritual resources insufficient to meet the minimum daily
requirements for anything like normal mental, spiritual and
emotional health and growth.

The would-be autonomous individual actually is an
unknowing parasite – he exists on what God has provided for
him in the created world, as well as on resources provided by
society. Only God is independent, self-existent, autonomous,
and this truth utterly shapes our relationship with him.

But who is this God we worship?

God and the Universe

'The god of the philosophers,' according to the great Blaise
Pascal is 'not the God of Abraham, Isaac and Jacob'. The
philosopher's god is 'the unmoved mover', 'the Absolute'.
He usually is not even a 'he', but an 'it' – an impersonal force
of some kind. The theology of Hollywood is expressed very
neatly by a sage Obi-wan Kenobe as he gives young Luke
Skywalker the benediction, 'May the force be with you.' But

the gods of secular philosophers and entertainers are simply projections of human imagination based upon nothing more than mortal knowledge, experience and wishful thinking.

Paul argues in Romans 1:19-23 that there is a true knowledge of God revealed in nature; it is not, however, an adequate knowledge, and is easily distorted by those who trust in their own reason rather than in Scriptural revelation. So, Pascal was correct when he pointed out that the 'god' secular philosophers end up with is not the God of the Bible, but one inevitably made in their own image. Sadly, the same is true of the gods of the great world religions.

But the living God cannot truly be known simply by human reasoning and imagination, because he is entirely different from mankind and all our experience. God states he is immortal and beyond our perception: 'God, the blessed and only Ruler, the King of kings and Lord of lords, who alone is immortal, and who lives in the unapproachable light, who no one has seen or can see' (1 Tim. 6:16). Our God is eternal, and not part of his creation: 'Before the mountains were born or you brought forth the earth and the world, from everlasting to everlasting you are God' (Psalm 90:2). God is unique, the only real God: 'So that you may know and believe me and understand that I am he. Before me no god was formed, nor will there be after me' (Isa. 43:10).

God's revelation of himself begins with the very first verse of the Bible: *In the beginning, God created....* Even non-Christians can quote this verse, without having to acknowledge its truth. But these five words are absolutely fundamental to understanding both God and our relationship to him. This is how God tells us that he existed before he created the universe and how he continues to exist outside of creation. It tells us God *chose* to create, for his own purposes.

God does not *need* creation; he *wanted* creation. Thinking on this ought to be a profound encouragement to us.

Another glimpse into the self-sufficiency of God is provided in Exodus 3:14, when God not only speaks to Moses from a burning bush but introduces himself by the name we translate as Yahweh or Jehovah: 'I am what I am: I always was and always will be what I am.' The Hebrew says in effect, 'I am the God who is.' Now this is a strange name, certainly not one we would think of. But the Name itself is God's way of explaining himself, of his eternal existence above and beyond the universe in which we exist. The concept contained in the Name of God is completely beyond our limited experience.

All that we as creatures know of our physical universe has an origin. All our science is based on principles of cause-and-effect. Everything that is has a chain of cause preceding it. We are born because of the actions of our parents, who were born because of the action of their parents, who were born because ... and so on.

But God is without origin or cause – he just *is*. He always has been and always will be. There is no chain of events preceding him, quite the contrary! All that creation is can be followed back, link by link, to the Creator. He holds the chain, in fact. Self-existent, self-sufficient, self-contained, unlike anyone and anything else. 'There is but one God, the Father, from whom all things came and for whom we live; and there is but one Lord, Jesus Christ, through whom all things came and through whom we live' (1 Cor. 8:6).

Jesus said that the Father has life in himself (John 5:26) and that he as the eternal Son of God has life in himself (John 14:6). This is true only of the Triune God. Ultimately, God is the cause and source of all life because life exists naturally only in him. His own life is not derived or received. He is the Lord of all existence.

Some have said, erroneously, that God created himself. This is more than logically impossible, it is silly. For a 'self' to be created there must be a creator before the self. God did not invent himself; he was and he is. Our created, finite minds cannot fully comprehend this, but God has graciously given us an adequate understanding of the nature of our Creator.

God and Time

Your life in this world began at conception. Nine months later you began your independent physical life. Up to then, there was no 'you', nobody with your particular physical and emotional make-up, your fingerprints, your DNA. Humanly speaking, you did not exist before your birthday. Every human life that has ever been or will be comes into this state of being at a particular point in time, and from birth to death our existence is set within the framework of time.

God has no birthday. He alone of all beings did not 'begin' to exist at any particular point in what we call time. Moses in Genesis and Paul in Colossians both point out that before creation, God existed. God simply is not part of the process of time. His eternal nature does not just mean he has an infinite hourglass or a cosmos-sized calendar to check off the passing eons. It is crucial to understand that time is a tool God has made for his use, and for our benefit.

When he created the heavens and the earth, complete with sun, moon and stars, God was providing convenient means for humans to measure the cycles of days, months and years. Today's engineers set clocks to the ticking of atoms. Yet however we count time, our universe is subject to its relentless procession of moments. Only the Lord is free from and outside of time, for he created it. God is truly 'timeless', a case where less really is more!

Cartoons sometimes depict God as a kindly, bearded grandfather figure in the sky – a sort of white-robed Santa Claus figure, without a bag of toys. This shows complete ignorance of the fact that the aging process is confined, naturally, to time. Outside time there is no aging. The whole created universe is growing older, deteriorating, breaking down. Scientists call it 'entropy', the natural tendency for any system to run down and fall into ever-greater disorder – an inviolable law of physics which is conveniently ignored by members of the church of evolution.

Whether a footprint in the sand or a mighty mountain, all we know is subject to decay, in time. Except for God. He is neither old nor young. Revelation 1:8 says: 'I am the Alpha and Omega, who is and who was, and who is to come, the Almighty.' In Malachi 3:6 the Lord says: 'I am the LORD, I do not change.' God might adjust his methods of operating, but his nature and character do not change. He is outside of time, abiding in eternity. He is being worshiped now in heaven as the eternal, unchanging God: 'Day and night they never stop saying: "Holy, holy, holy, is the Lord God Almighty, who was and is and is to come" ' (Rev. 4:8).

The thirty times in the Bible that God is called the 'Living God' remind us that God cannot die. He always lives. Not only is God without a beginning, he has no end. He is indeed the Living God.

Some contemporary liberal theologians claim that God is part of his creation, bound up with the process of time, continually changing and being changed by the flows of time and circumstance. The Bible clearly says otherwise. God created time along with the physical world as an environment for us to exist within, not for himself. He is outside the limits of time and beyond the boundaries of the universe. He is the unique, eternal, holy God.

God and Influence

The heavens declare God's glory. Jesus Christ manifested God's character and brought glory to his Father in his life and actions. We honor and glorify God in our worship. But all this glory, whether shown in the heavens or in the life of Jesus Christ, is simply a revelation of what already exists. It is not to be thought of as 'adding' to God. He is neither greater nor less when his glory is revealed or when we give him the worship due his name.

Which is another way of saying we are not doing God a favor when we worship him. 'If you are righteous, what do you give him, or what does he receive from your hand?' (Job 35:7). We are simply offering a small tithe of the honor he deserves from his creation. Neither is God influenced by our behavior. His own behavior is determined solely by his own free choice. God knows and does what is right regardless of circumstance and events in this world. The wonderful words of the great hymn say it well: 'There is no shadow of turning with Thee.'

Yet this self-sufficient God does care for and love all his creation with the possessive love of a Creator. Just because we do not influence or control God does not mean he is indifferent to us or our circumstances – just the opposite! It is we who can never break free from his influence and control – and his love and care. The God who needs no support system is, we must recognize, our sole support in this existence he has created.

The purpose of our study is devotional, not philosophical. God's self-existence is difficult for us to understand, but the Lord has not revealed this truth just to tickle our intellect. He wants to arouse our hearts to worship him as he truly is. We should adore his perfect, self-existent character, not just worship him when he does something nice for us.

The spoiled child will be nice to his father and thank him for a present, but ignore the father when there is no gift. It is natural for us to praise and thank the Lord for what he has done for us in Christ and for the things he continues to do for us in providence. But we also need to meditate on God's majestic and glorious character and thank and praise him just for who he is. And yes, God's self-existence should cause us to worship and adore him every day.

> Oh, the depth of the riches and the knowledge of God!...Who has ever given to God, that God should repay him? For from him and through him and to him are all things. To him be the glory forever! Amen (Rom. 11:33-36).

Conclusion

The first fruit of human sin and rebellion is the assertion of autonomy – the claim to independence from God, the claim to be like God. A generation ago Frank Sinatra first sang, 'I did it my way!' Alfred, Lord Tennyson wrote, 'For man is man and master of his fate.' Similarly, W.E. Hensley stated, 'I am the master of my fate; I am the captain of my soul.'

When proponents of legalized abortion redefined the terms of the debate years ago by describing their position as 'pro-choice', they were asserting the humanist view that everything – even killing unwanted babies before their birth

– is a matter of personal choice. This is to argue that there are no objective standards or absolute norms. As the popular saying of the 1960s has it, if it feels good, do it.

The humanist philosophy is wrong because it ignores or denies the truth that creatures have a Creator. We are finite – we have a beginning and an end in time, regardless of any choices we make in between. It might not feel good, but we are going to do it – exist, that is – on the Creator's terms, not our own.

David wrote long ago: 'When I consider your heavens, the work of your fingers ... what is man that you are mindful of him, the son of man that you care for him?' (Psalm 8:3, 4).

The Mormon church teaches that God was once man and we too can evolve into being gods. Nonsense! The living God is uncreated and eternal and self-existent; we are his creatures. Not only that, but we have become sinful creatures. The only proper response for the child of God before the face of our self-existent Creator is to acknowledge complete dependency. As believers we live by faith in him, for we know that by ourselves we cannot do anything right in his eyes, but through his grace we can do anything he calls us to do. We renounce the foolish assertion of human independence and live in dependence on, and in fellowship with, the Lord who alone is free to choose.

Instead of boasting in our puny abilities, Christians should boast in his grace which liberates us to do right. We are those who 'worship by the Spirit of God, who glory in Christ Jesus, and who put no confidence in the flesh' (Phil. 3:3). We are concerned to glory not in ourselves, but in him who loved us and freely chose to allow us to know him by faith, and to live with him forever.

Questions

1. What does the term 'aseity of God' mean?
2. While Christians claim man is the creation of God, atheists claim that God is the creation of man. How would you refute this idea?
3. When a millionaire asserts that he is a 'self-made man', does this contradict or modify the doctrine of his creation by God?
4. God created man with what kind of relationship to himself?
5. Having made us, why did God allow humans to turn against him?
6. In what sense are humans parasites?
7. What comfort is there in knowing God to be self-existent and eternal?
8. Explain John 5:26.
9. Scientists talk about creating life in the laboratory; how is this different from God's creation of life?
10. What effects can be seen in modern society after a generation of public education that promotes human autonomy as a virtue?

Chapter Two

Why is there not Nothing?

The attribute of
Creativity

*In the beginning God created
the heavens and the earth* (Gen. 1:1)

In the beginning, God created. This flat, unambiguous statement is the core of all debate over creation and evolution, the idea that life and all of the physical universe came into existence entirely by random chance. Scientific data can be produced to support arguments both for and against theories of evolution. But evolutionary theory cannot answer the much more fundamental question of *why* there is something and not nothing. Or, if this universe is the result of chance, how then can such random origin result in such intricate harmony of design? Simply, before we discuss *how* this universe came into being and developed, we should ask *why* it ever came about in the first place.

Specific arguments for or against evolution are obviously beyond the scope of this study. It is worth noting, however, that after ignoring the great debate for too many decades – possibly fallout from twentieth-century cultural events such as the Scopes trial and the film *Inherit the Wind* – Christians today are more willing and better-prepared to defend the Genesis account and biblical creation. The case is helped when the public understands the details and implications of the theory of evolution that was presented as absolute fact in junior high earth science class. In fact, there are Christian apologists who enjoy deflating the increasingly speculative, even desperate, defenses of evolutionary theory by demonstrating that it actually requires a greater leap of faith to accept an evolved universe rather than a created universe!

The only answer to the question 'Why is there something and not nothing?' is that there is a Creator. We exist and the universe exists because we were formed by a wise, loving, and purposeful Creator. And one of his attributes is creativity.

Creation Requires a Creator

A basic principle of thinking in the ancient, pagan world was that the universe was immense and eternal, and that any gods were a part of it. All living beings were connected like links in a chain of being, with humans being one link somewhere in the midst of the chain and with the gods as the final links at the top.

These ancient ideas have resurfaced in our modern day, popularized as New Age thinking. The poem read by Maya Angelou at the 1992 presidential inauguration is a good example of today's pantheistic thinking, which claims that the universe flows out of God's being and is part of him. 'Process' theology similarly argues that God is part of his creation and necessarily influenced by it.

God's revelation of himself in the Bible makes it clear that he is not part of, nor influenced by, his creation. When God created, he did so out of nothing because nothing existed except God. He created all that exists by his own will alone. He commanded the universe to exist.

We naturally find this difficult to understand, because our experience shows we cannot create something from nothing. Fortunately, our Creator is not limited as we are, or limited to what we imagine him to be.

Henry Ford took thirty years of trial and error to make his first practical automobile. Today the factories that bear his name require only eighteen man-hours to assemble a new car that can be driven out the plant door. How is this possible? Because the knowledge, skills and resources of management and workers have advanced so far, just as that new car contains more computing power than the Mercury spacecraft that took John Glenn into space!

The resources, knowledge and skills of God are infinite,

not just by comparison but in fact. Any god with limits is not the living and true God. How can we know all this? Because God tells us so. God's creative activity is described all through the Bible, not just in Genesis: 'By faith we understand that the universe was formed at God's command, so that what is seen was not made out of what was visible' (Heb. 11:3); 'he spoke, and it came to be; he commanded, and it stood firm' (Psalm 33:9).

Why Did God Create?

God created because he is creative. What a wonderful truth! God had no need to create, he chose to. Why? Because his nature is creative. God takes pleasure in inventing and forming things and beings different from himself.

The Lord our God appreciates order and harmony and beauty and variety. What a richness is shown in the variety of creation! He even created the multicolored fish of the ocean depths that only he can see and enjoy in their element. A creative God did not stamp life out of a common mold. He surely is never bored, because his nature is to be creative.

> Lift your eyes and look to the heavens: who created all these? He who brings out the starry host one by one, and calls them each by name ... not one of them is missing ... Do you not know? Have you not heard? The LORD is the everlasting God, the Creator of the ends of the earth (Isa. 40:26, 28).

God puts thought and effort into the act of creation, and he never tires of bringing new creations into existence.

Of course, his greatest delight is taking sinful, sad, fallen creatures and re-creating them: 'Therefore, if anyone is in Christ, he is a new creation; the old has gone, the new has come!' (2 Cor. 5:17).

God could have chosen to do something else, but his creative energy led him to bring into existence our universe and ourselves.

What was his chief purpose? 'The heavens declare the glory of God; the skies proclaim the work of his hands' (Ps. 19:1). Here we have it. God's creation glorifies him. The order, harmony and beauty of creation reveals to his creatures something of his perfect being, and thus glorifies him in his works. The purpose of creation gives purpose to mankind, the highest part of that creation. We are to reflect his divine character and so give him glory.

What was his motive? *Love*. God chose to share his perfection with other beings – to give to angels and to mankind the pleasure of knowing him. All, out of love. It was love that placed Adam in a perfectly beautiful garden filled with the spectacle of an enormous variety of sensory delights. Along with this matchless physical beauty, God also gave to his created child the moral beauty of his holy and righteous character. Out of this pure love he created mankind with the ability to know and have fellowship with their Creator. There can be no greater joy and delight; and no greater sorrow than the loss of this fellowship.

Which is why when man fell into sin and lost the intimate knowledge of and fellowship with the Creator, God again used his infinite creative powers to make a way of salvation and a Savior – at an enormous cost to himself. No greater love exists than this. And in love God continues to reform and renew his people and shape them into the bride for his Son.

The standard of creation is the beauty of God himself, as the Psalmist tells us: 'One thing I ask of the LORD, this is what I seek: that I may dwell in the house of the LORD all the days of my life, to gaze upon the beauty of the LORD' (Psalm 27:4).

But what does the Psalmist mean by beauty? The question has been much debated, and not only in the context of Scripture. The great Greek philosopher Plato talked of measure and proportion. The thirteenth-century theologian Thomas Aquinas wrote of integrity, proportion and clarity. Today we tend to look for a lack of imperfections, or of harmony of form that pleases our senses. In 1996 a *Newsweek* cover story debated what physical beauty is.

Humans find beautiful those objects or people that give pleasure or satisfaction primarily to our senses of sight or hearing. Meanwhile philosophers argue whether objective beauty truly exists, or is something simply 'in the eye of the beholder'. Is beauty objective, or subjective? Yet the solution to this age-old dilemma is actually found in the source of beauty – in the nature and character of the living God who is the essence and source and summation of true beauty. The object of our worship and the subject of our adoration is the beauty of our God.

It is also important to recognize that this true beauty is not found in mere appearance. God is Spirit, without shape or form. So how can the Psalmist talk of the beauty of God? David was speaking of the Lord's moral excellence; his attributes of holiness, goodness, truth, mercy and love. His being, not his appearance, is morally beautiful.

This does not diminish the privilege of perceiving beauty within our physical world. In fact, this ability is enhanced by a deeper understanding of beauty as more than sight and sound. When we look on masterworks such as Rodin's *The Kiss* or Rembrandt's *Night Watch*; when we hear a Chopin nocturne or a Mozart symphony, or observe a Shakespeare drama, we do well to rejoice in the sensory pleasure of the work. But true delight comes from understanding that God created people to reflect his being, his moral excellence, in these physical terms such as order, harmony and proportion. All of mankind's 'creativity' reflects, at our limited level, the glorious creativity of God. Besides, what masterwork of human hand or thought surpasses the majesty of the sunrise, the awesome power of the thunderstorm, the delicacy of a nightingale's warble, and the controlled authority of a lion's roar?

Why Did God Create Mankind?

A vast block of marble was received in the city of Florence which no sculptor, save one, would touch because of a flaw in the stone. This one man built a fence around the piece of marble, erected a shack inside the fence, and lived there for two years. When his labor was complete and the fence had been torn down, the people of Florence gathered around, gazing in awe at the statue Michelangelo had wrought from 'flawed' stone. The work became known as the 'David' statue, one of the great artworks of the Renaissance. No one had seen the statue in the marble save Michelangelo; and no one but he had the ability to form it. To him is attributed a famous comment: 'I don't create my sculptures; I only uncover what is already there.'

When God created man, he took a special delight in his work because this living, thinking being was made in the image of God, to reflect the image of God. Nothing else in all of creation is given this unique honor. Our fallen, corrupted image does not give God pleasure. Yet he does take pleasure in loving us in spite of imperfections and sin, and in re-forming us according to the image and standard of the Lord Jesus Christ. When Jesus returns and the universe is renewed, when sin and imperfections are finally abolished, both God and man will rejoice together in their mutual reflection in the perfection and glory of heaven.

God created man so they could have fellowship with him. Not because the triune God needs more fellowship than is already enjoyed within the Trinity, but so that they might enjoy his fellowship in a creaturely way. That ideal fellowship was aborted by the Fall, but is being restored by our Lord Jesus Christ, one believer at a time. As we follow him, we can walk with God – at a distance for now, but one day hand-in-hand.

Because God is creative, we have so much to look forward to in this life and especially in heaven: 'No eye has seen, no ear has heard, no mind has conceived what God has prepared for those who love him' (1 Cor. 2:9).

In the lump of clay which is the child of God, the Lord sees the image of Jesus Christ which he has planted there. And he wants to form that image in you despite the flaws. Whether with your co-operation, or even against your will, he will achieve that purpose in you, for that is the reason you and I were created.

Creativity and You

The child of God should pause and worship God for his beauty, and for the beauty he has created. The beauty of God is revealed most clearly in the portrayal of his Son, Jesus, given to us in the Gospels. Most of us find it easy enough to praise our God for the wonder of his actions of love, but how often do we pause to contemplate the sheer beauty of Christ's character? The book of Revelation offers us the vision of the Lord Jesus sitting enthroned in glory and beauty and light and splendor and majesty, resplendent in perfection, surrounded by physical symbols of beauty such as jewels and gold, and being worshiped by angels and other spiritual creatures of strange and wonderful form, appearance and variety.

The Old Testament psalms are filled with appreciation of the wonder of physical creation (Psalm 96, for one example). We are surrounded by sunrises and storms, snowflakes and stars, the flora and fauna of field and hill, all of which should turn our thoughts to God in praise and thanks. How much we lose when we don't pause to reflect on the majesty of creation and the Creator!

Over lunch one day in Paris, in a cafe on the Left Bank, the great Rodin got into a friendly argument with fellow sculptor Bourdelle. His friend was rather depressed and declaimed that artists such as themselves were useless people, dreamers, that the world could do well without them. Rodin denied this and asked Bourdelle to consider the occupations of other people, to observe that most people worked only out of necessity and were happy to avoid labor as much as possible. Artists, Rodin claimed, set an example for the rest of mankind. 'How much happier humanity would be if work instead of a means of existence were its end ... for the word artist ... means to me a man who takes pleasure in what he does.'

While this rejection of work as a necessary means to an end was unrealistic, Rodin was indeed correct in noting that the more creativity people put into their labors, the greater happiness they derive from work. He might also have recognized that the more creative we are, the more we glorify God our Creator.

Although we cannot create out of nothing, we can emulate our Creator by being as creative as we can with our personal abilities and the physical resources of this planet. Genesis 4 states that Jabal developed farming, Jubal was the first musician, and Tubal-Cain pioneered technology. In Exodus 31, God provided creative talents to Bezalel and Oholiab to construct the most beautiful tabernacle in the world. We are not all equally gifted. But we all can do something creative and glorify God as we work on the tasks at hand.

A teacher showed me a brightly-colored design produced by a ten-year-old boy in her class. Smiling, she told me, 'Noah was devoted to this painting. He told me in detail how he conceived it and planned it. He returned to work on it whenever he could. In the morning he would rush into the room for just a second to check on how a particular color had dried, and ask me if I would let him come in some time during the day to work on it. His thoughts have revolved around this painting for days now. It is a gift for his father.'

I wonder how much more excellent in value and how satisfying to us personally would be our creations if we were as highly motivated to please our Father in heaven!

We can also use our creative imaginations to improve life for others. One person invented a prosthetic device that not only enables legless people to walk, but to run. One man using this device entered the Paralympics and ran the 100-yard dash in just over eleven seconds – barely two seconds slower than the world record holder! Creativity takes many forms, such as developing new methods of organizing workplaces to reduce the stresses of menial, repetitive, boring factory labor. And even the least gifted homemaker can find more productive uses of time and ability than watching afternoon soap operas. The ideal wife of Proverbs 31 demonstrated creative homemaking (even if we don't all have her household budget to work with). Christians can reflect the image of God by using their creative imaginations to improve the environment and make life better for themselves and others.

Even when we are not gifted in particular areas, we have the capability to enjoy the creativity of others. There is a false kind of piety in many churches which claims Christians should have nothing to do with art, music, film, or dance because they are 'worldly'. Nonsense! Sharing in the sinful attitudes, thoughts and desires of those hostile to God, that is what constitutes worldliness, and artistic creativity is not 'worldly' until it is applied in these contexts. Neither are things worldly; people are. The Bible says God gave us all things to enjoy in the right way. The basic principle is given in Philippians 4:8: 'Whatever is true, whatever is noble, whatever is right, whatever is pure, whatever is lovely, whatever is admirable – if anything is excellent or praiseworthy – think about such things.' No human product is totally good or totally bad.

Therefore, we must evaluate and discern, becoming critics in the classic meaning of the word. A Christian can admire the Taj Mahal, the Alhambra, or the Parthenon for the magnificent architecture, while deploring the false religious ideas that are associated with them. We can deplore the ugliness and distortion of God's truth in some literature and art even while we respect the talent or enjoy the skills being demonstrated.

There was a medieval Pope called 'Pope Trousers'. He earned this nickname when he had all the public statues in Rome covered with 'clothes' so that the populace would not be tempted by lust. This bizarre act flies in the face of the Bible's teaching that 'to the pure all things are pure'.

Christians are exhorted to 'judge righteous judgement' – i.e., to learn discernment in order to appreciate the beauty in all things, especially those things created directly by the Lord himself.

Christians are not called to live in grey buildings, sit on grey furniture, or look at grey walls! We are created with the ability, even the responsibility, of appreciating this multi-splendored world that God has created as our earthly home, in all its color, variety and harmony.

Questions

1. How would you answer a child who claimed that God created us because he was lonely?
2. How does the native American Indian belief in a 'Great Spirit' differ from biblical teaching?
3. Describe some evidence that shows the physical universe was purposefully and intelligently created, and is not the accidental result of some cosmic 'big bang'?
4. Which aspects of creation do you most enjoy? Which do you neglect?
5. Show from Scripture that God created out of nothing.
6. Is the theory of natural evolution consistent with divine creation?
7. What in your opinion is beauty?
8. Is it possible to enjoy created things too much?
9. How does God 'recreate' people?
10. How can you be more creative at work? In your home? In your church? In your neighborhood?

Chapter Three

Royal Freedom

The attribute of Sovereignty

Yours, O Lord, is the greatness and the power and the glory and the majesty and the splendor, for everything in heaven and the earth is yours. Yours, O Lord, is the kingdom; you are exalted as head over all. Wealth and honor come from you; you are the ruler of all things. In your hands are strength and power to exalt and give strength to all. Now, our God, we give you thanks, and praise your glorious name (1 Chron. 29:11-13).

The magnificent prayer of King David (see previous page) acknowledges that God has absolute authority and rule over every detail of the universe. God and only God is in control. Some years ago A. W. Pink stated that the sovereignty of God is the 'foundation of Christian theology ... the clear center of gravity in the system of Christian truth'. This is not a popular doctrine today.

All heresy results from some sort of over-emphasis. One aspect of truth is stressed to the point of denying another aspect of truth. All truth must be kept in balance.

Some orthodox Christians over-emphasize the truth of the sovereignty of God so that they become fatalists or hyper-Calvinists. The opposite danger is an over-emphasis on the responsibility of man, eventually denying the sovereignty of God. This fallacy is clearly the more widespread tendency in Western churches and society.

The biblical teaching on God's sovereignty is little understood and even less appreciated. To know God better, we must understand and appreciate this aspect of his character.

The Meaning of Sovereignty
Most Christians are by now familiar with the story of Joni Eareckson Tada, one of the best illustrations of God's sovereignty in our times. Joni was a teenager when she dived into a lake and broke her neck. When she realized that she would be paralyzed from the neck down for the rest of her life, Joni rebelled and cried out against God. But through the love and support of her family and the members of her church, Joni was able to accept that this was God's will, and that it was for a good and higher purpose.

Since accepting God's will for her life, Joni has been used by God to accomplish more good than most fully healthy people ever will. She is an author, a recording artist, has a syndicated radio program, even is a painter with the brush clamped in her teeth! She is married, and has even acted in a movie about her life. As Joni travels the country, she tells the crowds gathered to hear her story that 'I would rather be in this chair, knowing Jesus, than out of it, and not knowing Jesus'. And there is no doubt that she means it. God's ways are not our ways, but they are much better, whether we understand them or not.

Joni's example is one way of demonstrating a fundamental aspect of the relationship between God and his creation: the only truly free person is the one who knows, accepts, and trusts in the sovereignty of God.

'Sovereignty' means absolute authority and rule. God, the Creator, is in control of everything he has created. He is sovereign. He has a purpose and plan, and as he is almighty every event past, present and future happens because he has ordained it. Nothing can interfere with his purpose and plan.

Even the 'laws' of nature and of science do not function independently, but they operate in harmony and in accordance with his will. God is not only outside the laws of science, he controls them. This is why he also is able to alter and vary natural laws in our physical universe in accordance with God's purposes. We use the term 'miracle' to refer to the occasions when he does this, to events that contradict the 'laws' of nature as we know them.

Miracle has become just another word cheapened by casual use, to the point that today almost anything is called miraculous, whether the birth of a baby or finding a good parking place at the mall. It takes away from the awe we should find in recognizing a miracle as an open act of God done for our benefit and education.

Just as gravity is an act of God, so also the parting of the Red Sea was an act of God. Just as the passage of the seasons is an act of God, so also the feeding of the 5,000. Just as the movement of the planets is an act of God, so also the resurrection of Christ. God is in complete control of both the 'natural' and the 'miraculous'. He can allow people to act in a sense truly by themselves. He can also both harden the heart of a Pharaoh and soften your heart to believe on him.

When we pray to God, 'your will be done', we are to have no doubt it will be. God is sovereign. He has no rivals, tolerates none. This was the lesson Nebuchadnezzar learned the hard way:

> I, Nebuchadnezzar, raised my eyes towards heaven, and my sanity was restored. Then I praised the most high; I honored and glorified him who lives forever. His dominion is an eternal dominion. His kingdom endures from generation to generation. All the peoples of the earth are regarded as nothing. He does as he pleases with the powers of heaven and the peoples of the earth. No one can hold back his hand or say to him, 'What have you done?' (Dan. 4:34-35)

Why Sovereignty Is Not Appreciated

Why is God's sovereignty so seldom preached or even discussed in our churches? It seems the only time the subject comes up is in old hymns when we worship 'the King'. Why is this such a problem? Perhaps it is the idea of sovereignty itself, and our natural human reaction to it.

There are some characteristics of God that we cannot fully comprehend. His eternity, his self-existence, his triune nature; these aspects of God remain beyond complete human understanding, simply because we have no comparable experience or examples.

But sovereignty is different. We have no lack of comparisons or examples, from the emperors of antiquity to the dictators of our century. Even our Western democratic forms of government are, in one sense, another type of sovereignty. We merely exchange autocratic rule by a person or cabal for the rule of the masses; 'government of the people, by the people, for the people.'

And that is the rub. We understand sovereignty very well, because the craving of fallen man's heart is complete self-rule. We will fight to the death to be in charge of our existence (though we fight just as hard to avoid any responsibility for the outcome). Our desire for personal sovereignty runs head-on into the sovereignty of our Creator. God's sovereignty denies our autonomy, our asserted independence, our freedom to be our own master. And we don't like it. Even our political systems attempt to exclude and deny God's sovereignty over government, whether it is monarchy, socialism, or democracy.

In some churches we find a 'liberation theology', which calls us to seek freedom from unjust social structures and inhibitions. The problem is we also seek freedom from God's control and the inhibitions of his will. Our culture encourages us to exalt our freedom above God's sovereignty.

In the evangelical church the gospel call to repentance and faith is often reduced to an 'invitation' system, inviting sinners to 'consider' Jesus and then 'decide' for themselves, as if selecting just what size, cut, and color of salvation we would like tailored specifically for us. We attempt to form a partnership, instead of calling on God in faith for his mercy. It denies the complete lordship, or sovereignty, of God by implying that human beings are in charge of their own destiny.

We want to be in control. We have hated, rebelled against the idea of God in control ever since our first parents listened to Satan ask, in effect, 'Did God say that? If you ignore God's sovereignty, you can be gods too.' But God is sovereign because he is God and we are not.

So, then we debate the philosophical issue of a sovereign, good God and the seemingly contradictory presence of evil and suffering in his creation. Humans disobey God, they literally defy his sovereignty by asking: why does the Almighty allow this? When a terrible illness or disaster strikes our family, we ask: how can I believe a loving God is in control?

The biblical answer is because he has a hidden, long-term purpose in mind that we can only partially glimpse in the Bible. Although God's absolute authority is challenged, and mankind is allowed to defy our Lord, his sovereignty is not diminished in the least. God allows humans to disobey and act against his revealed will, while continuing to accomplish his sovereign purposes *through* human disobedience. This is a marvelous truth, perhaps as great an example of divine authority and power as any in Scripture. It is further verification that 'all things do work together for good to those who love God, those who are called according to his purposes' (Rom. 8:28).

But what of disaster, misfortune, personal tragedy? How can these things, often a result of no particular sin or disobedience, demonstrate God's sovereignty? The cancer, the automobile accident, the teenager paralyzed while enjoying a swim? Why would God allow Joni Eareckson to lose full use of her body for the rest of her natural life? Because God determined to use Joni to minister to many other suffering souls and bring greater glory to his name through her afflicted body than through her whole body.

Does this satisfy you? Of course not. In times of crisis, of great tragedy, the hurting heart often cannot – will not – accept this truth. Even in the good times we can rationalize all day long and still be unhappy with the doctrine of God's sovereignty.

There are two answers provided in Scripture. One is found in Romans 9:19-21:

> One of you will say to me: 'Then why does God still blame us? For who resists his will?' But who are you, O man, to talk back to God? Shall what is formed say to him who formed it, 'Why did you make me like this?' Does not the potter have the right to make out of the same lump of clay some pottery for noble purposes and some for common use?

Do you see Paul's argument? Who are you? Are you qualified to judge God? What folly! We are sinful, finite, and foolish. We can no more judge a holy, infinite, wise God than the ant can judge Einstein.

A second answer is in Revelation 21:1-5. There we are told of the glorious vision of our sovereign God finally abolishing all evil and suffering, and introducing his kingdom of righteousness and peace and joy. This is the certain future, guaranteed by the resurrection of Jesus. We as Christians live our lives in faith, trusting that God is good and his purposes for us are good. As is written in 2 Corinthians 5:7 (see also Hebrews 11: 1-2), we walk by faith, not by sight.

In the end – or rather, in the here-and-now – the sovereignty of God can only be appreciated by faith in his character as it has been revealed to us in Jesus Christ, especially when we consider the cross. We cannot appreciate it from the perspective of circumstances which do not make sense to us. How could we? It would be like asking for an ant's perspective of the Grand Canyon. Only from an eternal vantage point can the spectacular panorama of creation, and the sovereignty of the Creator, be truly appreciated.

Why Sovereignty Is Important

My wife and I had been in the United States for just three months when we ran out of money, and then out of food. I was studying in seminary and Christina did not yet have a work visa. The scholarship money we thought would last a year had lasted three months. Now we were broke. We had told no one exactly how tight things were; many other seminary students were in the same position. I will never forget sitting down that morning with my wife and asking God to provide us with food. I had recited the Lord's Prayer hundreds of times before without any doubt of its truth and relevance, but now I realized I really was asking for 'our daily bread'! Bidding Christina good-bye, I went off to my studies. It was a long day, and it was not easy to concentrate.

Leaving the Montgomery library on the way home, I passed Rev. Corey, the pastor of the church across the street from the seminary. He waved, shouted Hi, and I greeted him back. A few steps further along I again heard him calling, 'Hey, Ken, wait a minute!' I walked back and Henry Corey told me he was distributing some Thanksgiving gifts to some students, and he had one package left over. 'Here, take this,' he said cheerfully, and lifted a huge box out of the trunk of his car. It was packed with enough food to last us for weeks. Needless to say, I went home rejoicing and relieved.

But some time later, we ran out food again; and again we prayed for divine intervention. At the end of that same day I checked my seminary mailbox, out of habit, and found an envelope in it. Inside were 100 one dollar bills. There was no note, name, address, or anything but the money. To this day we do not know who was the human instrument in God's hand that was the answer to our morning prayers. But we knew for sure that God is in control of everything and everyone, and no one else is.

The sovereignty of God is the greatest comfort a Christian can have in time of suffering. Whether illness, bereavement, betrayal, or loneliness, it is vitally important for us to realize that God is in control of everything. Whatever our circumstances say, the truth is that God is the sovereign Lord. He will fulfill his purposes in us. When all else turns against us, God remains sovereign and greater than any set of circumstances.

The Devil is not in control of the world or of our lives – God is. He who is in us is greater than he who is in the world. This is important to understanding our circumstances, but also crucial in dealing with sin and temptation. Not only can we have victory over particular sins, but God's sovereignty assures us of ultimate victory. We can persevere in the Christian life with the confidence that God is sanctifying us to complete the work of salvation in us.

Finally, only a truly sovereign God can truly love us. This is comforting when we think about it: our rebellion against his authority cannot threaten God or turn him from his will. This is why God is able and willing to love the worst sinner and the lowest failure. There is no circumstance that can thwart his love. Because God is a loving sovereign, as we see at the cross, we can trust him and pray to him. Three of the most important and reassuring words in all the Bible are 'He is able'.

Consider these passages:

Hebrews 7:25: Jesus Christ *is able* to save completely all those who come to him.

2 Corinthians 9:8: God *is able* to provide all we need.

Ephesians 3:20: God *is able* to enable us to grow.

Hebrews 2:18: God *is able* to help us in temptation.

2 Timothy 1:12: God *is able* to keep all we have entrusted to him.

Philippians 3:10: God *is able* to transform our bodies.

Jude 24-25: God *is able* to make us perfect in glory.

Recently the newspapers carried an announcement by the Dalai Lama that the next Buddhist leader, the next 'little Buddha', had been found. He is an ordinary six-year-old boy, who is supposed to be the latest reincarnation of the Grand Lama. This custom has been followed for many, many years. Buddhist priests, guided by their horoscopes, scour the world until they light upon some child they feel is to be their next leader. No matter how lowly, how unattractive, this boy is declared at once to be the Grand Lama. Between the moment of his selection and his enthronement years later, he undergoes a long period of training during which he receives the dignity of his title and the reverence of fellow Buddhists.

Whatever we may think of this strange practice, it is indeed reminiscent of the sovereign manner in which God chooses his people and prepares them for their destiny in glory.

Conclusion

No wonder the psalmist says in Psalm 46:10: 'Be still and know I am God.' No wonder the angelic beings cry: 'You are worthy, our Lord and God, to receive glory and honor and power, for you created all things, and by your will they were created and have their being' (Rev. 4:11). No wonder Paul says, 'Who shall separate us from the love of Christ?.... In all these things we are more than conquerors through him who loved us' (Rom. 8:35-38). No wonder our gracious Lord Jesus commands us to be anxious about nothing. Praise God that he is indeed sovereign!

Questions

1. What do we mean when we say 'God is sovereign'?
2. Does your church teach that God is totally sovereign, or that God and man 'co-operate' in salvation?
3. If God is totally sovereign, why is it wrong to conclude that after conversion Christians do not have to do anything to get into heaven?
4. Why do you think God's sovereignty is an unpopular truth?
5. If we habitually worry, do we really believe that God is sovereign?
6. Why is the idea of a human sovereign a bad idea, and the idea of a divine sovereign not?
7. Are God's decisions in any way contingent on human decisions?
8. Could God have prevented the rebellion of Satan and the fall of mankind?
9. Recall an incident in your life when you realized fully your absolute dependence on God for the necessities of life.
10. If something like what happened to Joni, were to happen to you, are you certain you would respond with submission and faith?

Chapter Four

The Rock

The attribute of Immutability

I, the LORD, do not change
(Malachi 3:6).

As you sit with that first cup of steaming coffee on a cold morning, you open the newspaper. Your eyes might fall on a notice that a well-known scholar will lecture on the 'immutability of God'. Without a second glance or a glimmer of interest, you instead search the pages for the day's words of wisdom from those well-known philosophers Garfield and Snoopy, or if you are from the United Kingdom, from Andy Capp.

But when you attend a Christian's funeral and join with fellow believers in heartily singing 'On Christ, the solid Rock, I stand', you're saying essentially the same things that scholar would have said. The words and the context are more personal and meaningful, of course. But the academic phrase 'immutability of God' and the songwriter's image of Christ as our Rock speak of the same concept: our God does not change.

We live in a culture that values change, that equates change with improvement. We like variety; we admire progress. So it is not surprising that to the current generation the image of an unchanging God seems at least a bit old-fashioned, if not positively out-of-date. That is, until we stand at the grave side, sense the complete awareness of loss, and suddenly long for an immovable rock to cling to.

The unchanging character of God has been under attack, as indeed all truth has been. Some have said that if God does not change, then he must be inactive now and uninterested in this world and our lives. That was the image of the gods of mythology. They never changed, but their immutability meant they were static, immobile, uncaring, unmoved by human events. They were up there, humans were down here. What a source of discouragement this immutability was.

On the other hand, process philosophers deny the

immutability of God by saying he is constantly evolving into something more than he was. This god is always changing, growing much as humans do. This god is more like a plant, not a rock!

But what does the Bible say? James 1:17 answers: 'God does not change like shifting shadows.'

When we were children we may have enjoyed making animal images with our hands held in front of a light. The shadows cast on the wall could be a rabbit, turkey, dog, whatever. We could make the shadowy shapes jump, turn, fight or kiss each other. But when all the lights in the room were turned on, the shadows and the animals vanished.

Every day the sun rises and sets, every night the moon waxes and wanes, and as these heavenly bodies move through space they cast light on this earth, making shadows. These can be long or short, but they cannot be captured or kept. By definition they change and eventually fade from view.

Not so with God; unlike his creations he does not wax or wane, change, or disappear. He is the one constant.

When God identified himself in Exodus 3:14 as 'I am who I am', he told Moses something very important about his own nature. He always has existed and always will exist just the way he is. God is not evolving! The God who spoke to Moses is in every way the same God who had spoken centuries earlier to Abraham, and centuries later spoke to David, Elijah, Paul and Peter; and who speaks to you and me today through his written Word. The God we pray to is the same God they prayed to. He is no older nor younger, no better nor worse, no more nor less wise, and no more nor less reliable.

The book of Hebrews (13:8) says the Lord Jesus Christ 'is

the same yesterday, today and forever'. The same is true of
the Father and the Holy Spirit – the triune God who has not
changed and will not change.

As we come to God in prayer and read the Bible, we come
with the assurance that God is constant. If he is good, we can
count on him never to do what is bad; if he is omniscient, he
is never ignorant of anything in our lives; if he is
omnipresent, we will never be separated from him; if he is
loving, he will always work in our lives for the good.

God is not like we are. When was the last time you
struggled to make a decision, only to change your mind later
because your decision showed poor judgement? Do you feel
compelled to make choices based on incomplete
information? Have you ever lied rather than admit to a
mistake? God never uses poor judgement, never relies on
incomplete information, and never has to cover for mistakes,
because his judgement is perfect, his knowledge complete.
Thus, as we are told in Numbers 23:19: 'God is not a man,
that he should lie or change his mind.' This complete
knowledge and perfect wisdom is why we can know that
God is aware of all things and in control of all things.

God is unchanging in three ways in particular.

How God Is Unchangeable

First, God's *being* is immutable, unchangeable. As much as
we may preach or sing about the eternal God, we still fail to
entirely grasp the awesome implication of a never-changing
God. Consider that he is never more divine or perfect, or less.
All of his attributes and qualities remain the same, yet he is
neither static nor immobile. And although he is always
active, his actions do not alter his essential being.

The psalmist said of him: 'Before the mountains were

born or you brought forth the earth and the world, from everlasting to everlasting you are God' (Psalm 90:2). Further on in Psalm 102:25-27 we read: 'In the beginning you laid the foundations of the earth, and the heavens are the work of your hands. They will perish, but you remain; they will all wear out like a garment. Like clothing you will change them and they will be discarded. But you remain the same, and your years will never end.'

Second, God is immutable in his *character*. Just as his essential being does not change, so also his character cannot change. God is never better or worse morally, never more or less wise or kind or righteous. In his treatment of us in this century he is just as loving, just, and holy as he was with the people we read of in the Bible.

Here again God is different from us. People change, and not just physically. Our changes in character, for better or worse, are as certain as the changes in our bodies. Change isn't necessarily a bad thing, of course. If we say to our beloved, as Billy Joel sang, 'don't go changing', we are going to be either pleasantly surprised or sadly disappointed because there is going to be change, one way or the other. In fact, it would be tragic if we did not change through the years of shared experiences and circumstances. But God is utterly reliable because he and his character do not and will not change.

I met Dave and Jenny in the fellowship hall after a worship service. They were a few years older than I, and as we talked they seemed to be a wonderfully happy couple, if somewhat quiet. Eventually I asked how they had become Christians, and a strange thing happened. They became completely silent and looked at each other for a long time. Then, hesitantly, they asked if I really wanted to hear of their background. Well, by now of course I said that I did.

This was their story. They had grown up in a country church and been involved in the youth group for years. Church was just a normal part of life's routine. But the pulpit ministry was not very helpful – the pastor didn't seem to have much to say, and the sermons were rather boring so no one paid much attention. Dave and Jenny got married, just like their friends, and settled down into married life. Then the routine of their lives was destroyed by the death of their first child.

They compensated by throwing themselves into work and partying. They found their pleasure in food, drink, and one party after another. After some time they realized they had no more interest in the church, or even in God. They became uneasy about this as they remembered Bible passages such as 'it is impossible for those who fall away to renew their repentance' (Heb. 6:6) and 'they went out from us because they were not of us' (1 John 2:19). They began to fear the loss of salvation; was hell their destiny, had they committed the unforgivable sin? Their concerns drove them to study the Bible for the first time with real seriousness, and gradually they came to understand those difficult passages and to believe the gospel promise again that 'no one who comes to me will I reject'. Together they rededicated their lives to God – now with a real sense of gratitude and appreciation for the wonder of his love.

As they told their story I could feel the intensity of their devotion to the Lord and their quiet enthusiasm to serve him. In all their agonizing over the state of their souls and in all their doubts about God's willingness to receive them back, it was the realization of the immutability of God that gave them faith and assurance. The unchangeable nature of God is to Dave and Jenny the anchor of their souls.

Third, God is immutable in his *purpose*. He tells us through the prophet Isaiah: 'I am God, there is no other; I am God, and there is none like me. I make known the end from the beginning, from ancient times, what is still to come. I say: My purpose will stand, and I will do all that I please' (Isa. 46:9-10). There is no power in the universe that can cause God to change his mind. His purposes will be achieved for us and for his church, as in Isaiah 14:24.

God has no need to change his mind or his plans. We change our minds because we lack knowledge of the future, or our plans because we lack the power to carry them out. But God is completely different. God knows the future and is able to overcome any and all opposition or resistance to his plans. When events surprise you, they come as no surprise to God; they are a part of the outworking of God's long-term purposes for you as his child.

We must now examine statements in Scripture that seem to contradict the unchangeableness of God's nature, character and purpose.

Does God Change his Mind?

If God is immutable, why then does the Bible sometimes say God repented or changed his mind? Passages such as Genesis 6:5-7, Jeremiah 26:3, Joel 2:12-13 and Jonah 3:10 are sometimes used to argue that the Lord does actually change his mind or his plans.

In Genesis 6, when God saw what man had become, we read that he was sorry that his creation had degenerated and decided to destroy most of mankind. Was God altering his plan and his purpose for mankind? No. He altered his *relationship* with that generation of men, but he persevered with his purposes of salvation and blessing. And he still does.

God sent Jonah to Nineveh to fulfill the purposes of salvation to those Gentiles. The Lord promised destruction to the wicked city in Jonah's concise sermon: 'Forty days and Nineveh will be destroyed!' But when the people of Nineveh repented, God removed his threat and blessed the city. Did God's purposes change? No. His *relationship* with the Ninevites changed as a result of their change of heart.

So it is with other examples of God's 'changing his mind'. We must understand that language suited for describing human behavior is often necessarily applied to God. This 'anthropomorphic' language is figurative, not literal. 1 Samuel 15 says that God repented that he had made Saul king, which is a human way of describing the attitude and emotions of God. His purpose had always been to make Saul king for a while to teach Israel some lessons about kingship, and then replace Saul with David. He carried out that plan. But when Saul behaved wickedly, God was grieved and changed his attitude toward Saul from one of favor to one of rejection.

In other words, the change that the Bible describes in God is a change in his relationships with particular people, based on their responses to his will. It is also a change in his methods of working with people from time to time. But these changes themselves are part of his ongoing plan for mankind generally. All that he does is in harmony with his character and eternal plans.

God's purposes do not change. His actions do. How else could there be salvation? God's holy anger against unrepentant sinners changed to an attitude of tender love the moment they repented and believed. The righteous judge 'changes' to the loving Father, without altering him and his nature. What caused the change? God's eternal purpose to give to them, in time, the gift of grace and salvation.

> As for you, you were dead in your transgressions and sins, in which you used to live.... But because of his great love for us, God, who is rich in mercy, made us alive in Christ ... and God raised us up with Christ and seated us with him in the heavenly realms in Christ Jesus (Eph. 2:1-6).

God did not change; his relationship to us changed.

When Paul said that the Mosaic covenant had been abolished, he meant that God had done exactly what he had planned to do, although he had not revealed it with full clarity to Israel. Jesus Christ's coming to earth was the most radical, the most world-changing event in history, yet it had been planned from eternity, before there was a creation. When God intervenes in human history, when God acts in our lives, when God is creative, when he does something new or different, all that he does is still in complete harmony with his unchanging character, purposes, and plans. A father driving six children 600 miles in twelve hours will experience several changes in attitude and feelings along the way. But that does not (or at least should not!) alter his purpose to take everyone all the way to the destination.

Because God is immutable in his being, his character, and his purpose, we can say with Paul:

> Who shall separate us from the love of Christ? Shall trouble or hardship or persecution or famine or nakedness or danger or sword?... No, in all these things we are more than conquerors through him who loved us. For I am convinced that neither death nor life, neither angels nor demons, neither the present

nor the future, nor any powers, neither height nor depth, nor anything else that is in creation, will be able to separate us from the love of God that is in Christ Jesus our Lord (Rom. 8:35-39).

Conclusion

> When peace, like a river, attendeth my way,
>   when sorrows like sea billows roll;
> whatever my lot, Thou hast taught me to say,
>   'It is well, it is well with my soul.'

After the loss of his family and his business in one brief span of time, Horatio Spafford wrote these lines because he understood Paul's words in Romans 8:32: 'He who did not spare his own Son, but gave him up for us all – how will he not also, along with him, graciously give us all things?' God has proved his power and his love to us at the cross, and he will not and cannot change. No matter what happens in our changing circumstances, we can have peace in our hearts.

'You will keep in perfect peace him whose mind is steadfast, because he trusts in you' (Isa. 26:3).

Knowing that God is unchanging not only gives peace, but it helps us to trust him. If we can trust God for the forgiveness of all our sins, surely we can rely on him for all our other needs, for he has not changed. The psalmist says to God: 'You remain the same, and your years will never end.' He goes on to confess his faith: 'The children of your servants will live in your presence; their descendants will be established before you' (Psalm 102:28). So also Paul in Romans 8 writes: 'I am convinced ... that nothing can separate us from the love of God.' He was convinced of this by the immutability of God.

Because God never changes, we can pray to him with

confidence. Think of how he answered the prayers of Moses, of Daniel, of Elijah, of the blind beggar, of the Roman centurion, of Paul. God invites us to ask in accordance with his will and promises it will be given to us. James tells us: 'Every good and perfect gift is from above, coming down from the Father of the heavenly lights, who does not change like shifting shadows.' Because he is still in control of the heavenly lights and all the rest of creation, we can pray boldly and confidently for all our true needs and know that he will deal with us just as faithfully (if not always so spectacularly!) as he did with Moses, Elijah, and Paul.

The immutable God has responded to the prayers of his people many times in the Bible and in history by changing their circumstances or their hearts. God can change us and our circumstances; he has done it before, he can do it again, and through all these changes he remains the same, forever and ever. Amen!

Questions

1. What does 'immutability' mean?
2. Human character changes over time; why is this not the case with God?
3. In what three ways is God unchangeable?
4. If God does not change, how can he be sympathetic to us and respond to us?
5. Should our attitude to God ever change? Why, or why not?
6. What does the Bible mean when it states that God 'repented'?
7. Can God hide himself?
8. If God is unchangeable, what does this tell us about the Bible?
9. If disaster strikes you or your family or church, how does it matter that God is immutable?
10. What motivates you to rely on God?

Chapter Five

Awesomely Different

The attribute of
Holiness

Holy, holy, holy, is the Lord God Almighty
(Rev. 4:8)

There is a New Age ditty that goes 'Do not seek God in outer space; your heart is the only place in which to meet him face to face.' Or, there is the Krishnamurti poem: 'My search is at an end. In Thee I behold all things. I, myself, am God.' Which is nothing more than the offer Satan made Eve in Genesis 3. And yet another New Age author, Beverly Galyean, writes: 'Once we begin to see that we are all God, that we all have the attributes of God, then I think that the whole purpose of human life is to revive the Godlikeness within us.'

God is thus said to be in us all, or at least to be pretty much like us. We have seen how this cannot be true of the eternal, creative, sovereign, unchanging God. Yet the human face we try to fix upon God not only denies these attributes, it also denies his most central characteristic: his holiness.

The heavenly beings around the throne are not described as unceasingly calling out 'loving, loving, loving' or 'merciful, merciful, merciful', though this is entirely true of him. No, they endlessly praise the living God as 'holy, holy, holy'. He is absolutely holy. In this he is absolutely different from mankind. But what is the holiness of God?

The Idea of Holiness
The basic idea of the Hebrew and Greek words that we translate as 'holiness' is separation. Not merely goodness, but apart-ness. Genesis 2:3 says the Sabbath is holy – not that it is better than other days, but different, because God has deemed it so. The Temple was described as holy, meaning it had a different purpose from all other buildings. It was set apart for its different use as assigned by God.

The description of the Tabernacle in Exodus 40 provides an illustration of the meaning of holiness. The purpose of this portable structure, and the permanent Temple that followed, was to bring God close to his people. There they could approach God and learn his will and experience his presence among them.

The design of the Temple emphasized God's holiness because his presence was hidden from the casual view of the people. Three curtains separated humans from God. The first was between the courtyard and the surrounding camp of people; the second was between the Holy Place and the courtyard; and the third was between the Holy of Holies and the Holy Place. Each stage was increasingly holy, simply because it moved closer to the presence of God. No one could pass the third curtain and enter the Holy of Holies except one representative of all the people, the high priest, who was symbolically washed and purified before he was acceptable to represent sinful people.

God is separate from us because he is utterly different from us. Since he is absolutely pure and free from sin, he cannot be approached hastily or easily by sinful man. Yet even before sin had entered creation, the holy God was separate from what he had chosen to create. The Lord is not just better than man or greater than man, he is infinitely above those who were created in his image. When we pray 'Hallowed be thy Name', we are praying that the name of God will be used differently from all other names, because he is different from all others. His very name represents his character – his different, holy character.

Aspects of Holiness
Some people are attracted to New Age thinking because it seems to them that the biblical God is somewhere far away 'out there'. Because they find this distance causes an uneasy

sense of being alone in the universe, they try pulling this God down to their level, to be comforted by the idea that he or it is just part of them. God is a bit better than us, but not so good as to make us uncomfortable with our human selves – more like a familiar neighbor or favorite uncle.

But the living God declares: 'There is no one like me, the Holy One, above creation' (Isa. 40:25). God is not just a better version of ourselves: he is transcendent, he rules over all visible and invisible things from on high. His holiness is something so different as to expose our ideas of righteousness as tawdry.

In thinking of the relationship of this holy God to the created world, we should remember four fundamental aspects of his holiness:

(1) *The holy God is a God of majesty, grandeur, and glory*. He is the supreme monarch over all reality.

(2) *The holy God is a God of righteousness*. His law is holy not just because it is good, but because it reflects his nature. Since God's nature is holy, his will is also holy and is supreme over all.

(3) *The holy God is a God of wrath*. This wrath is not an emotional anger, but an absolute hostility to all impurity, sinfulness, rebellion, and human self-centeredness. These qualities actually defy God's holy nature and oppose his purposes.

(4) *The holy God is pure in mind and will*. He maintains himself as holy, separate from all corruption and evil. God is jealous of his own name and reputation, and of our submission to him (Exod. 20:5).

In his relationship with the world, the holy God is separate but still in control of all that exists. The Holy Spirit is in our sinful world, touching our lives, but is no less holy for the constant contact. He is called 'holy' particularly to emphasize that although he dwells in the believer's heart he remains separate from sinful man, as well as from any other being or entity that is at work in the world.

The Meaning of Holiness

Purity is also an aspect of holiness. Hospitals, space agencies, and microchip factories spend billions of dollars to design and maintain 'clean rooms' that exclude microbes, viruses and dust that can contaminate their work. This degree of purity can be seen as a kind of 'holiness'.

In the Middle East it used to be common to observe craftsmen sitting in the bazaars at work fashioning silver ornaments. These men would take silver coins minted in America and Europe, and melt the dimes and shillings to cast as silver charms for sale to tourists. Their procedure was ancient. One by one the coins were dropped into more molten silver over the smelting fire. The man sat at his work fashioning the ornaments, getting up from time to time to inspect the melted metal and skim off the dross, the impurities that floated free from the pure silver. Back to the table for a while more, then up again to inspect the pot and remove more dross. Over and over, until there was no dross left floating on top. Only when the craftsman could see his face reflected in the silver as in a mirror did he consider the metal fit for his use.

Malachi knew this image well. He says God is also a refiner, and will continue removing the dross in us until we are holy ourselves, ready to be cast in his mold. His holy nature demands this, and we must expect it.

The holy God is separate and free from all impurity and imperfection. He cannot be in any way touched by sin (1

John 1:5). God hates sin because it is a contradiction of himself and all that he is. John says in Revelation 15:4: 'Who will not fear you, O Lord, and bring glory to your name? For you alone are holy.'

God in his holiness is also good and righteous. The law of God is holy because it expresses God's character and will (Rom. 7:12). When Paul says that true righteousness comes from above (Rom. 10:3), he is saying that God's righteousness is different from human righteousness. Not just better, but different because it expresses his own uniqueness, his holiness.

God's holiness is absolute; it controls and defines all his other attributes. This is why God's justice is holy, his wisdom is holy, his power is holy. His mercy to sinners is also holy.

I wonder if you have ever kept a journal, a diary? It used to be quite common for people to record their thoughts and experiences in a journal, not for publication but purely for their own benefit. They could learn about themselves and their spiritual growth, or look back and gain wisdom from past events and ideas. I wish I had done that when I was young. If I had, I am sure I would be a lot wiser now! One reason few keep journals these days is their concern for privacy; they do not want other people to know their secret thoughts and desires, and are afraid a diary could be found by someone.

This is the meaning of holiness: when something belongs to you and you alone, when it is totally private to you, then it is 'holy' to you. That diary becomes your 'holy' book. God's holy book is his alone; he authored it. It contains his thoughts which are different from yours and mine. Yet God has chosen to share his private thoughts with creatures like you and me. He invites us to read his journal, the record of his love for man.

Conclusion

How then do we respond to a holy God?

The natural person (the unbeliever) responds to a holy God in shock, in fear, in resentment and in rejection. A holy God is a threat to the sinner. The unbeliever naturally wants to believe in a kind, nice, grandfatherly God who will never judge him. A holy, just God is a threat to the natural man's desires for independence of thought and deed. So, every person prefers to invent his own God or gods that he can be comfortable with, gods that are tolerant of sin and evil, undemanding ... safe.

On the other hand the Christian's reaction to the holiness of God is awe, humility, worship, and obedience. Our first reaction may be similar to Isaiah's when he saw the Lord: reverential fear and awe at the majestic holiness of God (Isa. 6:5). Then, like Job, we bow in worship as we acknowledge his divine right to direct our lives, and we seek to serve, glorify and know him (Job 42:6).

Above all, the cross of Christ motivates the child of God to fall down in worship of our holy God. Jesus sanctified himself to God the Father's will, knowing that his will was the cross (John 17:19). The holy God turned away from his beloved Son on the cross as the fury of divine wrath against sin was poured out on him. It was for us that Jesus suffered and died and rose again.

The love of a holy God changes our response from fear to love, from shock to worship, from resentment to gratitude, from defiance to obedience.

God declares his born-again child to be holy in union with

Christ, separated by his wonderful love to belong to him forever. As saints by the grace of God alone, we gladly respond to his call to live lives of holiness as we complete our pilgrimage in this world.

The Christian naturally desires to live a holy life, but often is frustrated and discouraged by his or her lack of apparent success in doing so. Frequently this is due to inadequate or unbiblical notions of what a holy life looks like. We sometimes think of holiness as a Herculean task for which we are wholly unsuited. To put it in theological terms, we often jump in our minds from the truth of justification to a sort of do-it-yourself sanctification, without appreciating the fact and state of our adoption as children of God. So let us reflect for a moment on this amazing and exciting biblical teaching.

The apostle Paul was familiar with the story of God's confrontation with the Pharaoh of Egypt in which the Lord declared 'Israel is my first-born son' (Ex. 4:22). He was also familiar with the word of the Lord that came through Hosea: 'When Israel was a child I loved him, and out of Egypt I called my son' (Hos. 11:1). From his familiarity with this Old Testament adoption metaphor, Paul developed the concept of God's people as the adopted children of God. Just as God adopted Israel at the time of the Exodus as his corporate son (Rom. 9:4), so in New Testament times, explains the apostle, God constitutes those who are separated unto him and righteous through faith in his natural Son, Jesus, as his own adopted sons and daughters.

In the Roman law of *adoptio*, a son was emancipated from the rule of his natural father and placed under the new authority of his adopting father. He was clothed in a new tunic which displayed his new family identity. He was given a tutor to guide him in his growth and to prepare him for his future role as a mature son of his adoptive father. From the moment of his adoption, the inheritance of the father was rightfully his one day in the future.

Writing to the Galatian and Roman churches, Paul developed this analogy of the Christian life. In union with their older brother, Jesus, in his life, death and resurrection, Christians have been adopted into God's family. They have been liberated from being sons of the devil and slaves of sin, to ownership by the Father in heaven (Gal. 4:4-5). He has clothed them in the righteousness of his own Son. He has given them the Holy Spirit as their guardian and teacher; his role is to lead them to God's word, teach them its meaning and train them in obeying it (Gal. 4:1-2). Sanctification, in other words, is the work of the Spirit, and the role of believers as obedient children is to submit to and cooperate with him (Rom. 8:14-15). He trains them to think and act like Jesus, the older brother. His presence in their lives is also the guarantee that the inheritance even now being prepared for them will one day be theirs for sure (Gal. 4:5-7). They cannot enjoy it until they are completely conformed to the family likeness, but when through death they enter into the family estate, that family likeness and its attendant inheritance will indeed be rightfully theirs.

The Christian's adoption as a child of God is a present reality but the enjoyment of all its privileges is a future reality (Rom. 8:23). 'He chose us to be blameless in his sight. In love he predestined us as his sons through Jesus Christ' (Eph. 1:4-5). Therefore the apostle exhorts believers to holiness in the following terms: 'Do all without complaining or arguing, so that you may become blameless and pure, children of God without fault in a crooked and perverse generation' (Phil. 2:14-15).

The greatest practical help I know to living a life of holiness is to appreciate not what you have to *do*, but who you *are* – in Christ. You are a child of the living God! God is your wise, merciful, kind, gracious, loving Father! You are not what you *feel* yourself to be, you are what he has *made you to be* – his very own son or daughter. Remember in the time of temptation or suffering who you are – who God the Father made you to be – his own beloved child.

'Come out from among them and be separated from them (holy) says the Lord ... I will be a father to you, and you will be my sons and daughters, says the Lord Almighty' (2 Cor. 6:17-18). The call to holiness is a call to uphold the divine family honor and live like a true child of God the Almighty Father.

Praise God that he is holy and that we will one day be free from all sin, and holy, as our Father in heaven is holy!

Questions

1. What does the term 'holiness' mean?
2. What is so wrong with the idea that God lives in everyone?
3. How did the Old Testament temple teach God's people about his holiness?
4. Why does our culture despise holiness?
5. How can you 'set apart Christ in your heart'?
6. How can humans become holy in the sight of God?
7. Does the modern 'seeker-oriented' church convey God's holiness in its worship services? Does yours?
8. Is personal holiness in part measured by our food, drink, clothing, denomination, or work?
9. 'Take time to be holy' says an old hymn. How?
10. What motivates you to become holier?

Chapter Six

Comprehensive Knowledge

The attribute of Omniscience

Nothing in all creation is hidden from God's sight
(Heb. 4:13).

O Lord, you have searched me and you know me.
You know when I sit and when I rise;
you perceive my thoughts from afar
(Psalm 139:1-2).

Inside the wire enclosure on the edge of the playground stood a young girl. Pressing herself into the farthest corner, she desperately tried to hide in the shadow of the school building from the gaze of other children as they filed past. She was being punished in front all her schoolmates this way, because she had proved immune to other forms of discipline. But this method worked. In the days following her brief stint in this public detention area, this formerly disruptive child became scrupulously careful of her behavior. She desired to avoid that public humiliation.

Most of us hate to be stared at. We're concerned about our physical appearance, we try to always dress properly, and we want to be well thought of. But more than that, we live in fear that people might look behind the appearance, that what we are inside will be exposed for all to see. We not only hide behind doors and clothing; we put on masks to keep people from knowing us a little too well.

God knows us as we are.

Inclusive Knowledge

Hebrews 4:13 tells us nothing is hidden from the Lord. Proverbs 15:3 says the eyes of the Lord are everywhere, watching the wicked and the good. We cannot understand just how God is able to know and see all things, because our own knowledge and vision are limited. God is omniscient.

One of my professors was the famous F.F. Bruce – famous not only for his huge scholarly output and godly character, but also for his prodigious memory. One evening we invited him to dinner, and as he sat at the table he glanced at our old set of encyclopedias on the bookshelf. His eyes lit up and he exclaimed, 'I see you have old *****' – that last part I did not understand, so I asked him what he had said. He explained that he was reciting the titles on the spines of the ten volumes according to a mnemonic device he had concocted as a child.

You see, Bruce had read the ten volumes of this encyclopedia as a child, and he recounted how he had found an error in the date of Prince Edward's wedding. He then described the volume, page number, column and paragraph in which the mistake was to be found! That was when I discovered that F.F. Bruce could remember accurately just about everything and anything he read, and the man read prodigiously. I have met a few other people since with 'photographic' memories, and have always been moved to envy. Yet, how small is their knowledge when compared to omniscience!

The Lord knows every detail of the physical world, from the smallest creature on earth to the furthest galaxies that man can observe. We can nod and agree with that truth a bit more easily than we accept that the Lord also knows the most minute details of our lives. And, the Lord knows everything that is in our minds and hearts. Our intentions, imaginations, our dreams, our secret sins, and yes, our love for him.

> You discern my going out and my lying down; you are familiar with all my ways. Before a word is on my tongue you know it completely, O LORD (Psalm 139:3-4).

> He knows the way I take (Job 23:10).

> He knows how we are formed. He remembers we are dust (Psalm 103:14).

> I know what you have in mind (Ezek. 11:5).

Search me, O God, and know my heart; test me and know my anxious thoughts (Psalm 139:23).

Lord, you know I love you (John 21:17).

Nothing can be hidden from God. The darkest corners are as open to his sight as the light. There are no secrets and no surprises, no knowledge that is beyond him. And, neither does the Lord forget. He can never be victim of memory loss! With humans some things are better off forgotten – a perfect, comprehensive memory would be an unbearable burden for us. But not for an infinite Lord.

Instantaneous Knowledge

The complete, inclusive knowledge of God is also instantaneous, always present with him. Because God is not bound by time he is aware of all things past, present, and future. He does not have to catch the evening news or scan the morning paper to add to his infinite knowledge. There is nothing to add!

This of course is completely different from human knowledge, which is sequential. That is, we understand events in their relationships to other events, how they developed from what they were to what they might become. We learn bit by bit, piece by piece, building a chain by linking what we know already with new knowledge. And naturally some bits and pieces become confused or lost – forgotten – and the chains become tangled. Or we try to pick up the chain somewhere in the middle and thus cannot know where it came from or where it is going.

But to God the past, present, and future are one. He lives in the 'eternal present' and knows what is to be as completely as he knows what was. God holds both ends of the chain.

This is why God could give prophecies in the Old Testament and accomplish them perfectly later in human time. Past, present, and future are one great activity that he controls and has perfect knowledge of. No one knows the date of the return of Christ, except the Father in heaven (Mark 13:32). He knows the date because he has decreed it.

We do not fully understand this because our minds are finite. Only in the infinite mind of God is all knowledge instantaneous.

Intuitive Knowledge

Not only are all things known by God at once, but his knowledge is also without effort. He does not have to learn or study. We develop by observation, by imitation, by trial-and-error, and by rational thinking. God knows. He has no need for observation or experimentation, because God's knowledge is intuitive. This is true because God knows himself, completely and accurately. Now, we do not automatically have true knowledge of ourselves, and we spend our lives denying much of what we do know. God knows who he is in a way we cannot.

He knows independently and immediately not only himself, but also his creation. Recall how God addresses Job from the whirlwind: 'Who is this that darkens my counsel with words without knowledge? Brace yourself like a man; I will question you, and you shall answer me. Where were you when I laid the earth's foundation? Tell me, if you understand. Who marked off its dimensions?' (Job 38:2-5). God was doing much more than putting Job in his place; God was reminding mankind exactly who he is.

Again in Isaiah 40:13-14 we are told of God's intuitive knowledge: 'Who has understood the Spirit of the Lord, or instructed him as his counselor? Whom did the Lord consult to enlighten him, and who taught him the right way? Who was it that taught him knowledge or showed him the path of understanding?'

God does not need to learn or increase his knowledge. He knows intuitively, comprehensively, and accurately.

Instructive Knowledge

Because God knows, man also can know. Psalm 139:6 says: 'Such knowledge is too wonderful for me, too lofty for me to attain.' Now although we cannot attain the complete knowledge God has in himself, we can attain that knowledge he has revealed to us to guide us. Only by following his guidelines will our knowledge be true knowledge.

We live in a culture that claims there is no need of God to understand the world we live in, that we can discover its truths by ourselves. Scientists and philosophers have been in the forefront of this notion. The idea that God has revealed knowledge to us or that there is anything we cannot learn is naturally offensive, even threatening, to this world view. These scientists and philosophers will often deny sinful human bias and subjectivity, which is the cause of the bizarre and foolish ideas that are popularized by the famous and adopted by the gullible.

Calvin described the Bible as 'spectacles' provided by God. It is an apt comparison. When we observe the world in the light of our own limited reason, our knowledge is correspondingly blurred and limited. When we look at the world in the light of the Bible, everything comes into focus and shows its true form and colors. We see clearly and gain true knowledge. We learn to think God's thoughts after him. We know because he knows.

Intimate Knowledge

There is one other aspect of God's knowledge we should know – it is intimate. Where the omniscience of God is threatening to the unbeliever, this personal knowledge comforts his children. He knows us.

Jesus said: 'Your Father in heaven knows what you need before you ask him' (Matt. 6:8). God knows our needs because he knows us better than we know ourselves. 'The Lord knows those that are his', just as an earthly father knows his own children, their personalities, character, strengths, and weaknesses. The difference is, God's knowledge of his children is perfect.

To unbelievers at the Day of Judgement, Jesus will announce: 'Depart from me, for I never knew you,' meaning that he had no personal relationship with them in their earthly lives. But to his children he will say, 'Welcome home.' In John 15:15 Jesus declares: 'You are no longer slaves, you are now my friends.'

Our knowledge of God is partial and faint. As Paul said, we see through a dark glass. But God's knowledge of us is complete, perfect, and intimate. When our sins are completely forgiven and we are clothed in the righteousness of Christ, we need not fear this terrible, complete knowledge of ourselves. Rather, we can rejoice in it! Whatever the world, the flesh, or the devil can accuse us of, our Father knows the truth: in Christ, we are beloved!

What Do You Know?

Human knowledge is always incomplete and partial. We know things by observing, studying and thinking, and it takes effort to learn. Yet even with all our best efforts we will never know anything with absolute accuracy unless we receive and accept the help of the Bible. The Lord has graciously given to us in his Word the principles by which we can observe the world and ourselves, and come to an accurate knowledge of what we see and experience. The Word of God indeed provides the spectacles we need to overcome the blindness and biases caused by sin's effects on our minds.

Through the Bible we can obtain accurate (though not total) knowledge of God's character, God's actions in human history, and God's will for our lives. We can learn the meaning and the purpose of this universe, what has gone wrong and how it is all being put right. We can even come to know ourselves.

Over and over, the Lord in Scripture commands us to 'know that I am Lord'. As God's people obey his Word, we develop a personal knowledge of God, not just of the truth about God but a personal relationship with him. We come to know him as Saviour, as a great God, as a faithful master, and as a loving friend. We learn not only to believe his Word, but to trust him completely.

Questions

1. 'God is omniscient' – what does that mean?
2. Is it difficult for God to know everything?
3. Does God know all that is possible as well as all that is real?
4. Where does God get his knowledge?
5. Can we know ourselves as God knows himself?
6. Can the believer know people and things truly and accurately?
7. How much of his knowledge has God made known to us, and how?
8. May a Christian ever say 'nobody understands me'?
9. How can we get to know God better?
10. What motivates you to become more knowledgeable about God, the world, the Bible, yourself?

Chapter Seven

The 'How-To' God

The attribute of Wisdom

To God belong wisdom and power;
counsel and understanding are his
(Job 12:13).

We live in a culture that places little value on wisdom. An entertainer draws a vastly larger audience than a wise person. No one wants to be thought of as a fool, but neither do most people try to be wise. Perhaps we confuse wisdom with a high IQ, or with conceited individuals who make a show of their knowledge. Or, we restrict wisdom to the province of gurus camped on mountaintops.

But knowledge and wisdom are two different things. Knowing facts and data is certainly a worthy pursuit, but wisdom is praised throughout Scripture as priceless. Proverbs 8 invites us to listen to God's wisdom and become wise ourselves: 'Does not wisdom call out? Does not understanding raise her voice?... To you, O men, I call out; I raise my voice to all mankind... you who are foolish, gain understanding... for wisdom is more precious than rubies...' (Prov. 8: 1,4,11).

What is the only source of true human wisdom? Job tells us it comes from God.

The Nature of Wisdom

Wisdom is one of the essential characteristics of God; all he does manifests his perfect wisdom. But, what is wisdom? In Exodus 31:1-6 we read that Bezalel and Oholiab had 'wisdom' in their craftsmanship, meaning they were skilled in that particular area. Wisdom is given credit as the source of the shrewd economic practices that make a person wealthy: 'I walk in the ways of righteousness, along the paths of justice, bestowing wealth on those who love me and making their treasuries full' (Prov. 8:20-21). Wisdom also results in good government: 'By me kings reign and rulers make laws that are just' (Prov. 8:15). One example is Solomon, as described in 1 Kings 5.

Wisdom is not merely knowledge. It is the right use of knowledge. Wisdom may be defined as the art of choosing the best ends and the best means of achieving those ends. Wisdom pertains more to skill than to information. Wisdom requires making the right choices and doing the right things in the right way.

Let's compare knowledge and wisdom:

Knowledge is related to intellectual information.
Wisdom is related to discernment.

Knowledge is related to the mind.
Wisdom is related to both mind and will.

Knowledge is related to theory.
Wisdom is related to practice.

Although wisdom is often appreciated in Eastern cultures, the West traditionally has placed a higher premium on knowledge. We admire people with lots of knowledge – professors, economists, computer scientists – without realizing that they often may possess little true wisdom. In this age of equal 'rights', our children are taught that their opinions are as good as anyone else's. They are not taught to appreciate that some people are wiser than others. Should we then be surprised that our culture applauds the clever, the witty, the superficial (witness our entertainment and cultural icons), but disdains the wise and thoughtful? It is far easier to gather data than to cultivate wisdom.

In fact, even highly-educated people are often practically inferior to the uneducated when it comes to wisdom (MENSA, the high-IQ society, has more than its share of very brainy but not very competent people as members!).

One person comes immediately to my mind who illustrates this point well.

When I was a very young Christian I shared an apartment with a remarkable young man. The memory of his life still humbles me. Harry had an IQ less than half of mine. His work was very stressful, not because it was tremendously difficult but because Harry was diagnosed as manic depressive (or what is now designated as bipolar disorder), and suffered terrible mood swings. Yet, he somehow remained cheerful and seemed to spend every waking moment, when he was healthy, helping others with their much smaller problems. Young people in the church came to him rather than going to others smarter than Harry, because he listened so well and always came up with a helpful response.

The secret of Harry's wisdom was simple. He used to get out his well-worn Bible every evening, go down to his knees, put his head in his hands, and study, study, study the Word of God. For *hours* he would stay there, sometimes rocking back and forth, often sweating. He would continue to prayerfully squeeze the truths of the Word out of its pages. In this state Harry was deaf to any interruptions, afloat as he was on the ocean of divine wisdom. Over time I became aware of Harry's ability, with his slow mind and halting speech, to express such wisdom and understanding. But, why should I have been surprised? Does not wisdom come from the God who promises, 'Seek wisdom and you shall find it'?

God's wisdom is controlled by his righteousness. We can appreciate his wisdom to some degree because we were made in his image, but God's wisdom is vastly higher than human wisdom and completely beyond our reach. Our wisdom is foolishness compared to his.

Who would not revere you, O King of the nations? This is your due. Among all the wise men of the nations and in all their kingdoms, there is no one like you. They are all senseless and foolish.... (Jer. 10:6-12).

However, God's wisdom is accessible to us through his Word and by his Spirit.

How and where, then, do we see God's wisdom?

God's Wisdom in Creation

When we observe nature we are often moved by its beauty and sometimes by its terrible power. But the universe also reveals the wisdom of God through the relationships of all parts of creation – their dependence upon one another, the interconnection – as well as through the marvels of individual creations. The human eye, the common ant, the Grand Canyon, the DNA code, all are marvelous demonstrations of the matchless skill of the Creator.

All things reveal skill in their making, because God is a how-to God! What he makes works, works together, and benefits us in the ways it works even if we do not yet understand it all. It was the poet Ogden Nash who quipped,

> The Lord in his wisdom made the fly;
> and then forgot to tell us why.

God knows why. 'By his understanding he made the heavens, his love endures forever' (Psalm 136:5). 'By wisdom the LORD laid the earth's foundations. By understanding he set the heavens in place' (Prov. 3:19). The Bible is filled with exhortations to examine and consider the details of creation as well as creation as a whole. God is not at all nervous about man's poking, prying, and probing the innermost workings of creation, whether examining the genetic code or observing the farthest galaxies. The great astronomer Kepler in the seventeenth century said his duty as a scientist was to 'think God's thoughts after him' – to think about, appreciate, and explore the skill and the wisdom of God as revealed in what he has made. The wise contemporary scientist will agree, while the foolish scientist will scoff.

Do you ever gaze at the stars on a clear night and consider the intricate, majestic job God did in creating the heavens? Or when you see the brilliant colors of fish in a salt-water aquarium, can you admire the varied shapes and hues and the thought that went into their design? We don't know why God made these things as he did, yet we can still rejoice in the delights of creation. Psalm 104 is an expression of the psalmist's appreciation of God's wisdom in the marvels he sees. All of God's works are purposeful as well as delightful. So take time to appreciate God's wisdom as revealed in creation!

God's Wisdom in Providence

The LORD foils the plans of the nations; he thwarts the purpose of the peoples. But the plans of the LORD stand firm forever, the purposes of his heart through all generations (Psalm 33:10-11).

One of the psalmist's greatest joys is to look back on the history of Israel and see how the Lord in wisdom has overruled the plans of men and nations and intervened to rescue and bless his people.

The most famous example in biblical history is the deliverance from bondage in Egypt, as the plans of Pharaoh were overruled by the purposes of God (Exod. 1-14). In Romans 9-11, Paul traces the providence of God from Israel in history and concludes, 'O the depth of the riches of the wisdom and the knowledge of God! How unsearchable his judgments, and his paths beyond tracing out!' (Rom. 11:33). It is amazing to study how God's control of the world and of history has produced his intended desires, despite the contrary intentions of people and nations.

God's wisdom is seen in the quiet skill with which he intervenes in the unfolding events of life, no matter how insignificant or ordinary they may seem to us. In fact, to God there are no trivial events, and nothing is routine or random. Events occur in such a way that his plans are always accomplished and that good ultimately triumphs over evil. It is easier to see God's hand in the 'big' events, yet actually they are at the end of a long chain of 'routine' or 'trivial' things that led to a great result. Consider in our lifetime the fall of the Berlin Wall, the end of the Cold War, the fall of communism, the Gulf War, the events in the Middle East. No one expected these events, but God is in control. His subtle hand unfolded events over years to these spectacular conclusions.

You might have heard of Paley's watch theory. This clergyman likened the creation of the universe to the work of a watchmaker who makes a watch, winds it up, then leaves it to tick away unattended. It is an easy philosophical means of granting God credit for creation, then shoving him off-stage so we can rule the world ourselves without interference. This, however, is not how God relates to his world. God remains active in creation, both in the physical world and in the plans of men and nations, to achieve his purposes. His wisdom guarantees his success.

God's Wisdom in Redemption

In 1 Corinthians 1:18-25, the apostle Paul referred to the preaching of the cross as 'foolishness' to the unbeliever. The pagans of Paul's day, and of ours, scoffed at the idea of human transformation through the suffering and death of a Jewish peasant in the shameful manner of crucifixion. Nor could the Jews believe the living God could live on earth and submit to the cruelty and injustice of the Romans. It is only through faith that Christians can see the cross is the wisdom of God. It is God doing the impossible to achieve the best ends: satisfying his own holy standards while freeing the slaves of sin from their just punishment.

Only our 'how-to' God could have conceived the substitutionary atonement and carried it out. It is the most amazing example of wisdom – even of God's wisdom – that exists. No human has such wisdom. To most unbelievers God's way of salvation looks like foolishness. But actually it is human wisdom independent of God that is true foolishness.

God's plan for our salvation, his slow preparation for it in the history of his Old Testament people, and his coming to earth himself to rescue us is true wisdom! 'In him we have redemption through his blood, the forgiveness of sin, in accordance with the riches of God's grace that he lavished on us with all wisdom and understanding' (Eph. 1:7).

God's Wisdom in the Church

God's wisdom is revealed in the church. Judged by many of our local congregations, this may be hard to believe! Often the church itself is seen as the great barrier to belief, and some say they would believe in God if the church were different. What they mean of course is, if the *people* in the church were clearly different from the world around them.

But 'his intent was that now, through the church, the manifold wisdom of God should be made known to the rulers and authorities in the heavenly realms' (Eph. 3:10). The many-faceted wisdom of God is revealed to the *angels* through the church! Not having the perspective of the angels, we cannot always see God's wisdom. But as we look back through the history of the church we can see some of God's wisdom.

God has glorified his name by accomplishing his purposes through people who are weak, sinful, and sometimes confused. Even when Christians have engaged in carnal conflict, God has advanced his cause. We can only marvel at the growth of the church and the salvation of millions through its often-feeble ministry. As one commentator wryly noted, the power of the gospel ought to be obvious, because it has survived so much bad preaching!

We can also see the wisdom of God as he uses the church to heal the sick, to comfort the bereaved, to encourage the weak, and to reconcile those in conflict. Only in and through the church is the love and compassion of the Savior seen by the world. The church is his light, illuminating the world. This is the wisdom of God, which is beyond our wisdom. The church is God's theater where his drama of victorious grace is played out now for the admiration of the angels, and will be later on for us in heaven.

God's Wisdom and You

God alone is truly wise. He knows how to do right things well. We are all influenced by the world's 'wisdom' which is the opposite of God's wisdom. By studying God's wisdom revealed in creation, providence, redemption, and the church, we can grow in wisdom.

When Miss Rogers told the class to write about someone in their family they admired, Tina knew what she wanted to say. 'My grandpa loved everyone and went out of his way to help people in need. People respected him and came to him with their problems because they knew he would listen quietly, and then give good advice. Grandpa always knew what to say. When I fell down he kissed my hurt knee and told me he loved me. When Grandpa said that, I knew he meant it. In my preteen years I was overweight, and suffered a lot of pain from the comments my classmates used to make about me; Grandpa would hug me and tell me God loved me no matter what I looked like, and always would, and so did he. Grandpa's wisdom shone through everything he said and did. He always knew what to say. Even when he didn't say anything, I felt a peace when I was around him.'

I find it touching that a young woman still has such contented confidence in the wisdom of an old man. Yet how much greater still should the believer's confidence be in the wisdom of the all-wise Creator!

Daniel praised God, saying:

> Praise be to the name of God forever and ever; wisdom and power are his. He changes time and seasons; he sets up kings and deposes them. He gives wisdom to the wise and knowledge to the discerning. He reveals deep and hidden things; he knows what lies in darkness, and light dwells with him. I thank and praise you, O God of my fathers: you have given me wisdom and power, you have made known to me what was asked of you... (Dan. 2:20).

God's people have always worshiped him in response to his wisdom. We may especially meditate on our future worship of God, which angels are even now experiencing:

'Worthy is the Lamb who was slain, to receive power and wealth and wisdom and strength and honor and glory and praise!' (Rev. 5:11-12).

Although we cannot in this life become as much like God as we wish, we can think his thoughts after him as we study and meditate on his Word. And we can begin to behave more like our Lord Jesus, who came to show us wise behavior. All of his human purposes and methods were right, good, and pleasing to the Father. Our skills of wise conduct in this world will develop and mature as we follow Jesus and his example.

The fear of the Lord is the beginning of wisdom. The love of Christ is the expression of wisdom.

Be very careful, then, how you live – not as unwise, but as wise, making the most of every opportunity, for the days are evil. Therefore do not be foolish, but understand the Lord's will (Eph. 5:15-17.)

Questions

1. What does it mean to say that God is wise?
2. What is wisdom and how does it differ from knowledge?
3. Where is the place to start if we want to become wise?
4. Describe some of the evidence in creation that shows God's wisdom.
5. Is it possible to be foolish and have a Ph.D.? Explain.
6. Can true wisdom be acquired from the public education system?
7. How valid is the media portrayal of Christians as ignorant, gullible people?
8. How does the cross demonstrate God's wisdom?
9. Why does the apostle Paul say not many wise people are called to salvation?
10. What is your motivation for becoming a wiser person?

Chapter Eight

The Righteous Judge

The attribute of Righteousness

Will not the Judge of all the earth do right?
(Gen. 18:25)

A professor of English at a Christian college recently published a book, not about his field of expertise in English literature, but about his daughter. This bright, happy, talented girl had graduated from college and was looking forward to a life of serving the Lord in nursing. A few days after her graduation, she was killed in an automobile accident. Trying to make sense of his daughter's death, the professor began writing down his thoughts, which eventually became a book.

This was far from the first book written by a grieving, searching heart for the same fundamental reason: attempting to understand how a righteous, loving God can allow painful things that often appear to be arbitrary. More simply, is God always fair?

Even Abraham asked this question directly of his God when confronted with the pronouncement of doom for the wicked cities of Sodom and Gomorrah: 'Will not the Judge of all the earth do right?' (Gen. 18:25). But Abraham asked the question in a very different tone of voice than an unbeliever would use. Abraham's argument contained in this simple question is, 'How could you, O Lord, treat the righteous and wicked alike?' The Lord is not an egalitarian! It is monstrous to think that the Lord would treat the good and the bad the same! What Abraham was really asking was that the Lord be consistent in his judgement and discriminate between good and bad – and of course, the Lord did just that.

All of us have struggled at times to understand what God's righteousness really means, based on our experiences of watching the rain fall and sun shine on the just and the unjust alike. It is indeed a difficult truth. God cannot be unrighteous – but, what does righteousness *really* mean?

Pagan Righteousness

A Jewish folk tale goes like this. Once a Rabbi decided to test the honesty of his disciples, so he called them together and posed a question: 'What would you do if you were walking along and found a purse full of money lying on the road?' 'I'd return it to its owner,' said one disciple. 'His answer comes so quickly, I must wonder if he really means it,' the Rabbi thought. 'I'd keep the money if nobody saw me find it,' said another. 'He has a frank tongue, but a wicked heart,' the Rabbi told himself. 'Well, Rabbi,' said a third disciple, 'to be honest, I believe I'd be tempted to keep it. So I would pray to God that he would give me the strength to resist such a temptation and do the right thing.' 'Aha!' thought the Rabbi. 'Here is the man I would trust.'

Biblical righteousness is not the same as righteousness from a humanist perspective, which is based on the premise that humanity is basically good and, therefore, has the ability to develop good moral behavior. People in the ancient world often believed that genuine righteousness was available and evident in nature or society. That is, guidance and instruction were found naturally in the world around them.

Plato taught that righteousness was to be found in a well-ordered society in which everyone kept to his station and performed his proper functions. In other words, righteousness was civilized behavior conforming to the status quo. This particular view of righteousness has been popular with many cultures at various periods in history, such as the fondness of Victorians for 'moralistic' teaching. And today even some Christians equate righteousness with moral behavior, with being civilized, polite, not being too different from the cultural norms, not showing too much enthusiasm so as to rock society's boat. Taking righteousness too seriously risks making your neighbors and your co-workers feel uncomfortable, after all.

Well, the Bible teaches that true righteousness is not to be found in this world, or in cultural consensus. It only comes down from above. As we are reminded in Romans 3:10, there is none righteous; no, not one.

Biblical Righteousness

Defining righteousness is surprisingly difficult. How would you define human righteousness? If you assert that it is measured by our conformity to the character of God, you are correct. But, how can we know that we *are* conformed to God's character? Is it measured by simple obedience to his law? In a sense, yes.

But the error that the Jewish religious system fell into by Jesus' day was that equating righteousness with law-keeping eventually decayed into the idea of merit, of *earning* the favor of God. Christians, too, often slip into a similar mind-set of merited favor based on our good deeds. The apostle Paul and other New Testament writers properly denounced this as heresy, a denial of God's unmerited favor we call grace. Make no mistake, God's law *is* necessary for us to know his will for our lives; but properly understood it addresses *internal* attitudes as well as *outward* actions. Therefore, the law cannot be kept perfectly, and we all fall short of true righteousness.

One of the most celebrated American folk tales is the story of young George Washington and the cherry tree. Whether there is any historical basis to the tale, the real interest to me is not the actions of young George but what is revealed about the *father*. There it resembles the parable of the prodigal son. The elder Washington had a fine orchard with a variety of fruit trees, including a particular cherry tree he had had imported. This tree received special care and nurture until it was ready to produce fruit. Young George is supposed to have gone out one day to try out his new hatchet, playfully chopping away at everything in his path – including his father's pride and joy, the famous cherry tree. Indignant, Mr. Washington searched for the culprit until young George was asked if he knew who had done this. George is reputed to have replied with the famous words, 'I cannot tell a lie, father. I did it with my hatchet.'

George was sent to the house to await his father, who rebuked him sternly for his carelessness and thoughtlessness. But then Mr. Washington added, 'I am sorry to have lost my cherry tree, but I am glad you were brave enough to tell me the truth. I would rather have you truthful and brave than to have a whole orchard of the finest cherry trees. Never forget that, my son.' And the boy who became the great man did remember this lesson from a wise father who valued moral righteousness more than possessions. In much the same way, we are to understand that our Father in heaven also values personal integrity and righteousness more than simple legalistic conformity.

But how can you measure God's righteousness? Is it defined by how well he obeys his own laws? Is God's law above God?

There were ancient Greeks who did believe that law was above God; some still believe it, such as deists. They claim God cannot perform miracles, because that would violate the very laws God created and is bound by. God himself could not behave differently from the ways his laws require us to behave. Is this true?

Of course not. Recall the sovereignty of God, his

knowledge and wisdom. His laws were given to his people at different times for our guidance, not his. The Lord our God is not the servant of laws he has created. He is the sovereign dispenser of laws that reflect his character, not the maker of rules that limit his actions. God is holy, separate from sin, and thus his actions are just. This internally and eternally holy nature results in righteousness of character and action. So then, is God's law less than righteous, is it arbitrary and amoral? No, because God is righteous in every expression of his character, including his law.

To grasp God's righteousness as expressed in his law, we must first understand the biblical teaching concerning the covenant relationship. The God who enters into a covenant with his people is not first a lawgiver, but a loving, holy, spiritual person. As such, he created man in his own image to have fellowship with him. When sin violated the created relationship, God made a covenant relationship between himself and his chosen people.

In that bond between God and man, God pledged himself to be kind and faithful to man, and required that man be faithful and loyal to God. To define the relationship more clearly, God has revealed various forms of this one covenant of grace throughout human history. In every form of the covenant – with Abraham, Moses, David, and the Lord Jesus Christ – God told us of his responsibilities to us and ours to him. Meeting our responsibilities brings blessing, breaking the covenant results in cursing. Specific blessings and curses added to the original form of the covenant God made through Moses with the Old Testament church are listed in Deuteronomy 28. In 1 Corinthians 11 Paul refers to blessing and cursing in the age of the New Covenant in relation to the Lord's Supper.

The righteousness of God is his faithfulness to the terms of the covenant, both in blessing and punishing, in providing for us and forgiving our sins. We must never forget, *God keeps his promises of the covenant*. He destroys the enemies of his people, and he makes his people prosper. Here is God's righteousness displayed in keeping the covenant with us. 'The LORD loves righteousness and justice; the earth is full of his unfailing love' (Psalm 33:5). God holds himself true to his own character and to the covenant of grace. He holds us true to his character also.

Righteousness is not merely conformity to rules and regulations, as many Jews and Christians have thought. It is conformity to the holy and just character of God, including the qualities of loyalty, mercy, trustworthiness, and kindness – in other words, the fruit of his Spirit in our lives. Because he is righteous, he always does what is right as defined by the many qualities of his perfect character.

We see God's righteousness only as it relates to his creation, especially ourselves. The Bible teaches two facets of divine righteousness: justice and salvation.

Righteousness and Justice

> Now we know that God's judgment against those who do such things is based on truth.... Because of your stubbornness and your unrepentant heart, you are storing up wrath against yourself for the day of God's wrath, when his righteous judgment will be revealed. God will give to each person according to what he has done (Rom. 2:2, 5-6).

The Lord's righteousness requires that he discriminate between the good and the wicked. This was Abraham's prayer in Genesis 18. It was Solomon's prayer in 1 Kings 8:31-32:

When a man wrongs his neighbor and is required to take an oath and he comes and swears the oath before your altar in this temple, then hear from heaven and act. Judge between your servants, condemning the guilty and bringing down on his own head what he has done. Declare the innocent not guilty, and so establish his innocence.

God's justice demands that the wicked be punished, not absolved or ignored but dealt with justly: 'The wrath of God is being revealed from heaven against all the godlessness and wickedness of men who suppress the truth by their wickedness' (Rom. 1:18). The writer to the Hebrews talks of 'a fearful expectation of judgment and of raging fire that will consume the enemies of God' (Heb. 10:27). The alarming failures of contemporary legal systems are absent from the court of divine justice toward which we are all traveling.

In the Old Testament, God often came with accusations against his apostate people (e.g. Hosea 4:1; 12:2; Micah 6:1-2). Then he carried out his condemnation of those who were unrepentant. This is God's retributive justice. The anger of a righteous God is aroused against sin, and justice exercised against the sinner.

Yet the retributive justice of God is balanced and even outweighed by his remunerative justice, by which he rewards his people when they are righteous. It is not because we deserve reward or merit favor, but because God is gracious and kind. Remember, God does not always punish; he often forgives. He shows compassion and rights wrongs.

One thing God has spoken, two things have I heard: that you, O God, are strong, and that you, O LORD, are loving. Surely you will reward each person according to what he has done (Psalm 62:11-12).

The injustice and unrighteousness that God tolerates now will be finally punished when he judges the world in righteousness. On that day of judgment, the Lord will defend and acquit his people of all accusations against them, just and unjust, on the basis of the righteousness of Jesus Christ that is given us through faith in him.

Righteousness and Salvation

When we consider salvation, God's righteousness is truly mysterious. Our human concept of righteousness basically means obeying the law of God in external ways. Justice in our terms requires that law-breakers be punished. The result is we seek to avoid punishment more than we desire to be righteous.

But the righteousness of the Lord actually *demands* that some guilty sinners be acquitted, forgiven, and saved to live with God forever. How can this be, that righteousness forgives the unrighteous to satisfy righteousness?

Because of his sovereign love, God gave his own Son to satisfy all righteousness for sinners, and he gave Christ's own perfect righteousness to us as a free gift. The cross is the supreme demonstration of God's righteousness, where he himself came to die in the place of the wicked so that they could become righteous and thus glorify him forever. We call this justification. God's righteousness actually demands that this occur!

The justification of sinners through faith alone is the ultimate expression of both the righteousness of God and his love. We are made fully righteous and acceptable to God only by his sovereign and free love.

Understanding that the only hope of true righteousness on earth was the Messiah, the Old Testament prophets longed for his coming: 'This is what the LORD says: Maintain justice and do what is right, for my salvation is close at hand and my righteousness will soon be revealed' (Isa. 56:1). The face of Jesus Christ, as he died on the cross in our place and rose with eternal glory and beauty, reflects the righteousness of God. The New Testament proclaims with triumphant joy that Jesus Christ is our righteousness!

The righteousness and justice of God are not just a fearful threat to us as sinners; they are our *only hope* in life and in eternity.

> The gift of God is not like the result of one man's sin: the judgement followed one sin and brought condemnation, but the gift followed many trespasses and brought justification. For if, by the trespass of the one man death reigned through that one man, how much more will those that receive God's abundant provision of grace and the gift of righteousness in life reign through that one man, Jesus Christ (Rom. 5:16-19).

Righteousness and You

Balaam prayed, 'Let me die the death of the righteous' (Num. 23:10). But Paul reminds us that there is no one truly righteous in God's sight. Human righteousness is hopelessly flawed by sin – by impure motives, by selfishness. Humans have to re-define righteousness down to a standard that they think they can achieve, though of course they fail to reach even that tawdry mark. As the Bible clearly states, we are slaves of sin and cannot make ourselves righteous by law-keeping, by having good intentions, or by exercising our willpower. The sad truth that we are and will always be incapable of making ourselves righteous will never be a popular truth.

The good news is that God himself has come down to

earth in the person of his Son Jesus, who lived a perfectly righteous life. In his earthly life we see true human righteousness as well as divine righteousness. When repentant sinners believe that God accepts Christ's righteous life in place of our disobedient life, the Father accepts us as we are in our new faith-union with Jesus. His righteousness is given to us so that we appear in God's holy sight as truly righteous: 'But now a righteousness from God, apart from law, has been made known.... This righteousness from God comes through faith in Jesus Christ to all who believe' (Rom. 3:21-22).

The adopted children of God are able to enjoy the fruit of the Spirit's presence in their lives – peace, joy, hope, confidence. Through the power of the Spirit of Jesus, who indwells them, they are able to overcome the sin in the old nature and in the world around them. The Spirit-filled life is the result of being made righteous in God's sight through the gift of Jesus' righteousness. Obedience to God now is no longer motivated by the fear of judgment, because that judgment has been meted out on the Son of God. Obedience now flows from the joyful heart of a forgiven, righteous sinner.

Questions

1. What does divine righteousness mean?
2. If God is righteous, why do wrong and bad things happen?
3. Does God hold everyone accountable to be righteous?
4. Are there any righteous unbelievers?
5. How does a person become righteous, as defined by God?
6. What would a righteous society look like?
7. Why is self-righteousness such an ugly human characteristic?
8. God's righteousness demands what sort of conclusion to world history?
9. Do people regard you as a righteous person? Why?
10. What is your motivation for living a righteous life?

Chapter Nine

How Good is God?

The attribute of Goodness

You are good, and what you do is good;
teach me your decrees
(Psalm 119:68).

The Bible says less about the goodness of God than we might expect. Biblical writers do not offer abstract discussions of various qualities and virtues, such as goodness or the nature of the good. In fact, they make it clear that goodness is not a theoretical issue at all. Accordingly, the Bible does not attempt to define goodness in terms of what human beings do or say.

'Good is what people desire,' asserted Socrates. But in Scripture, goodness is derived not from human character, but from the divine character.

Thus when the Bible does speak of goodness, it is of the goodness of God as it touches our lives through his providence, love, lovingkindness, grace, compassion, patience. These are aspects of the goodness of God as he relates to us.

God is Good
God is good in himself. That is, he is inherently good. It is his nature, which cannot change. In fact, you might say that God cannot help being good, because he is essentially good. This is one aspect of his perfection.

Now, we use the word 'good' in all sorts of ways and settings. To describe an object as 'good' can mean that it is useful to us, or attractive, or gives us pleasure. An action is 'good' if it serves our desires or needs. People are 'good' if they meet certain standards of action or character. 'Good' thus becomes a point somewhere on a scale.

This is not what we mean when we say God is good. God is *absolutely* good, regardless of what value we assign to him. His goodness is not a matter of good-better-best, or even the highest measure on the scale. His goodness is the standard.

The unbeliever accepts the idea of a good God if he provides some benefit. A man told me that as a young boy he prayed for a new bicycle for his birthday. When his desire was not met, he simply stopped believing in God. We might smile at this as the theology of a child, but is it really so different from our adult reaction to the promotion that never comes, or the loved one who chooses another spouse? Even Christians often define the goodness of God only in the terms of how it benefits us. But God is goodness personified, regardless of how he relates to us.

We also use the word 'good' in referring to a good athlete, a good gardener, or a good carpenter. In this sense we are commenting upon their skill or expertise in a defined area. Now this certainly does apply to God, because he is the expert at what he does. His work is indeed excellent, because he is the best! This good God also rules the world well and wisely.

There is yet another meaning for 'good'. A good man is an ethical person who knows the difference between right and wrong, who practices the right and rejects the wrong. In this sense God's goodness is revealed in his righteousness, justice, truth, faithfulness, consistency, and purity.

So there we have it. In both aspects of 'goodness' – skill and moral excellence – God is absolutely good. He is good in action and character, and only he absolutely and truly is.

Jesus said to the rich young ruler: 'Why do you call me good? No one is good except God alone' (Mark 10:18). Jesus was trying to correct this man's view that goodness came from keeping the law, by telling him that true goodness is found only in God. Only God is truly, absolutely, and completely good. Thus Jesus invited this young man to take a deeper look at him, to judge him with a new understanding of what good really meant, and then decide if Christ was as absolutely and fully good as God the Father. This would be a very different kind of goodness to look for than that of human moral actions.

God is truly good. We can always improve, always get better, but God cannot improve. He doesn't need to. He is the standard.

God is Good to Us

The goodness of God can be expressed through his benevolence to us. Here we find the Bible's teaching easier to understand, that God does what is good for us.

> The Lord is good to all; he has compassion on all he has made.... The eyes of all look to you, and you give them their food at the proper time. You open your hand and satisfy the desires of every living thing (Psalm 145:9, 15-16).

The Creator is benevolent to his creation, and that means to the unbeliever as well as the believer. Sometimes we Christians begrudge that his rain falls on the just and the unjust, but we should be careful. Even when we believers are ungrateful and take his goodness for granted, God continues to shower his goodness upon us. His benevolence extends to those who hate him.

Because God is good, his creation is good, his decrees are good, his laws are good, his providence is good. Paul reminds us: 'Why do you show contempt for the riches of his kindness, tolerance, and patience, not realizing that God's kindness leads you towards repentance?' (Rom. 2:4). The goodness of God should never be taken for granted, but should result in changes in our own lives. Let us consider some of the ways God expresses this goodness to us.

Goodness in Providence

God provides for all the needs of his children. We are blessed to have food, clothing, housing, jobs, friends, health, talents, possessions, time, and so much more. But he does more than provide for our needs, he allows us the enjoyment of his provision. The God who gives our daily bread also gave us taste buds to enjoy the flavor of fresh-baked bread and cookies. His creation is beautiful, and he has given us sight to delight in the beauty. These added gifts of God are not strictly necessary to live in this world; it is the goodness of a good God who provides these things for our pleasure.

This world is affected and afflicted by sin and corruption, thus there is sorrow and suffering. But more of good than bad exists in creation. In God's goodness, his full wrath is being held back until the Day of Judgement. This, too, is the goodness of God: 'I will establish my covenant with you: never again will all life be cut off by the waters of a flood' (Gen. 9:11). God is good and keeps his promises. His providence to all mankind is good, but it is especially so to his chosen people: 'He fulfills the desires of those who fear him; he hears their cry and saves them' (Psalm 145:19).

Goodness and Love

God's love arises out of his essential goodness. All human beings experience the providence of the Creator, yet not all are sensitive to his wonderful love. His adopted children are able to experience this love in many ways, the greatest of which was described in John 3:16: 'For God so loved the world that he gave his only beloved Son so that whoever believes in him shall not perish but have everlasting life.'

The love of God has been described as wide and deep and high. It is so great that it demanded the sacrifice of his own

Son to the death of the cross, in order to redeem us and introduce us to the eternal goodness of our glorious Lord. 'God demonstrates his own love for us in this: while we were still sinners, Christ died for us' (Rom. 5:8). This is the amazing thing – that the goodness of God leads to the salvation of sinners, and that those he saves, he prepares for glory.

Goodness and Lovingkindness

> The LORD is good, a refuge in times of trouble. He cares for those who trust in him (Nahum 1:7).

We have noticed already in Romans 2:4 that the lovingkindness of God is intended to lead us to repentance. The psalmist says: 'Because your love is better than life, my lips will praise you' (Psalm 63:3). This is his lovingkindness – the abiding, tender, reliable, covenant love of God expressed in actions. His lovingkindness is better than life itself. 'THE LORD, the LORD, the compassionate and gracious God, slow in anger, abounding in love and faithfulness, maintaining love to thousands, and forgiving wickedness, rebellion, and sin' (Exod. 34:6). In the midst of all their trials and difficulties, believers through the centuries have experienced this lovingkindness under both covenant administrations. Simply, the Lord is good and kind to those who trust him.

Goodness and Grace

Perfection is the standard for entering heaven, and perfection and goodness are not the same thing. We have seen that only God is perfectly good. Humans may strive to be good, but perfection is beyond us, and the realization that only perfection will satisfy a holy God is often painful to accept.

Jeremy Crawford writes: 'When I learned the difference between being good and being a Christian, I had a hard time with it. You see, my grandparents were all dead, and it hurt me to think that they might not all be in heaven. My grandmother and grandfather on my mother's side were strong Christian people; but my father's mother, to my knowledge, was not a Christian. She was a special woman, and people called her "good"; but there was no evidence that she trusted in Christ for salvation. She seemed content to trust in herself. It is hard for me to think that someone I loved might be in hell now; but if we do not realize the difference between "good" and perfect, then we are in big trouble.'

Grace springs from the essential goodness of God, and is his means of providing his goodness to us through Christ. It is a goodness undeserved, which cannot be earned, and is received by those who know they are guilty and corrupt.

Even before the cross there were examples of the favor God is willing to show to those he loves. God looked at mankind in the time of Noah and condemned it, but 'Noah found favor in the eyes of the LORD' (Gen. 6:8). Proverbs 3:34 tells us that God gives grace to the humble, but resists the proud.

The classic passage here is Romans 5:15: 'The gift is not like the trespass. For if the many died by the trespass of the one man, how much more did God's grace and the gift that came by the grace of the one man, Jesus Christ, overflow to the many!' The vivid imagery of the verse portrays the goodness of God as literally overflowing in generosity as God pours out his grace upon guilty sinners. And, this gift is given in far greater proportion than the trespass which preceded God's grace.

To quote Paul again:

> Praise be to the God and Father of our Lord Jesus Christ, who
> has blessed us in the heavenly realms with every spiritual
> blessing in Christ. For he chose us in him before the creation of
> the world to be holy and blameless in his sight. In love he
> predestined us to be adopted as his sons through Jesus Christ,
> in accordance with his pleasure and will – to the praise of his
> glorious grace, which he has freely given us in the One he loves
> (Eph. 1:3-6).

All that is good in you and me is by the grace of God
alone. 'Grace alone' was the watchword of the Reformation,
and it remains ours today. The good God desires to make us
good also, and grace is the means by which we can be
presented before him, blameless and perfect.

Goodness and Compassion

An aspect of God's goodness that we all should be familiar
with is compassion. It relates to his actions towards us in our
circumstances.

The compassion of God is his goodness expressed
towards those who are in distress:

> Praise be to the God and Father of our Lord Jesus Christ, the
> Father of compassion and the God of all comfort, who
> comforts us in all our troubles, so that we can comfort those in
> any trouble with the comfort we ourselves have received from
> God (2 Cor. 1:3, 4).

Many, many things in life that are meant for our ultimate
good do not feel good at the time, and stretch the limits of our
understanding of God's goodness. During these trials, it is
only the comfort and compassion of our Father in heaven
that will keep us going forward in faith. The ultimate cries of
the heart – 'Why? Why me? Why this?' – are heard in

heaven, and he ministers to our spirits out of his goodness and compassion.

Many years ago in language school in Germany, while waiting for my wife to join me there, I experienced God's goodness in a remarkable way. A fellow language student, a Turkish girl called Ismet, showed a strong interest in learning about Christianity. We had several conversations about religion, focusing on the identity of Jesus Christ as the eternal Son of God. Naturally, as a Muslim, she found this concept difficult to accept.

One evening as we sat and talked outside her house, she invited me in for further discussion. I happily agreed, sensing an opportunity to deal with her strong objection to the account of the cursing of the fig tree by Jesus. 'No holy man would do that!' she had asserted. So I followed her up the stairs to her room, and immediately became rather uncomfortable; the room was maybe eight by ten feet and contained a chest, chair, bed, and basin. She sat on the bed and I stood at the door, trying to concentrate on my explanation of the sovereignty of Jesus as Creator over his creation. Suddenly Ismet leaped off the bed, lunged at me and grabbed me about the knees in a vice-like grasp, and cried, 'Make me a woman!'

Looking back, I imagine it appeared pretty silly. But at the time I was literally paralyzed with shock. What should I do? How do you flee the temptations of the flesh when you cannot move? Several different thoughts and feelings flashed through my mind as I listened to her tell through her tears that she was 28-years-old and had never slept with a man, that she wanted to know what it was like, that no one would ever know since it would be just this one time, and so on.

I did not feel lustful, but I did feel something I would

never have imagined. It was a feeling of compassion for this girl that actually caused me to want to satisfy her desires, however foolish. If I pushed her away she could scream rape and I would never be able to prove my innocence. And besides, when Ismet cried 'Make me a woman!', she had pronounced the 'w' as a 'v', sounding just like Marlene Dietrich in one of those 1940s movies. But here I didn't know my lines, all I knew was I was in trouble with no idea how to get out of it.

So after the initial moments of shock and confusion, I cried out in my heart to God, 'Father, help me, please!' I began to speak as calmly and rationally to this woman as I could. I explained that this was not a good idea, either for her or for me; and that we needed to talk about her situation calmly; that this was a serious matter, a matter of sin against God; that I liked her as a friend but no more; and so on. While she cried I talked gently and patiently, despite the panic within me, and after I don't know how many minutes she loosened her grip. I was able, still talking quietly, to ease myself out of the room and back down the stairs to the street. When I looked back, her eyes were dark and hard with anger, or disgust, or hate – I am not sure which. But as I returned to my own apartment that night I thanked the Lord for his goodness in getting me out of danger without a mark.

'As a Father has compassion on his children, so the LORD has compassion on those who fear him' (Psalm 103:13). The goodness of God towards those who fear the Lord is expressed in his tender compassion. We need never feel lost or alone or helpless. He cares for us more than we are capable of caring for anyone. God is good.

Goodness and Patience

God's justice may demand punishment for the wicked, but his goodness results in divine patience with them: 'Why do you show contempt for the riches of his kindness, tolerance, and patience...' (Rom. 2:4). Under the old covenant God exercised his patience until the time of Christ: 'In his forbearance he had left the sins committed beforehand unpunished' (Rom. 3:25).

Paul had good reason to appreciate the merciful patience of God that he had experienced. How good God was in allowing Saul of Tarsus for a time to oppose his will and persecute his people, in order to bring him to salvation at the right time and subsequently reveal his glory through this man's grateful and powerful lifelong ministry! 'I was shown mercy so that in me, the worst of sinners, Christ Jesus might display his unlimited patience as an example for those who would believe on him and receive eternal life' (1 Tim. 1:16).

We might not have persecuted the Church, but all of us have offended the goodness of God. How good God is to us in bearing with our sins and failures as he gradually and patiently trains us in faith and righteousness! The Father is indeed still patient and long-suffering with his children.

Conclusion

God's providence, love, lovingkindness, grace, compassion, and patience are some of the ways that the essential goodness of his character are expressed to us and experienced by us. God indeed is good, and is also good to us. In fact, we would find the almighty power of God terrifying if not for the controlling presence of his essential, absolute goodness. How thankful we should be!

It is tragic that most people, even many Christians,

grudgingly acknowledge the goodness of God only on occasions such as Thanksgiving in the United States, or harvest festivals in other countries. This is directly opposite to the life of *continuous* thanks that should be openly evident in the life of a believer. All life owes its existence and thanks to God the Creator; the Christian should constantly give thanks to the good, gracious God of salvation.

Understand, believers are to abound in thanks always no matter what our circumstances may be, simply for the cross of Christ. Every time we consider our sin, we should immediately give thanks to God for the forgiveness he brought to us with the cross. When we slip into depression, we should remember that we have been adopted as children of God through the cross. When we are fearful, or defeated, we should cling to the resurrection power of Christ that is available to us since the cross. When the apostle Paul considered the greatness of the salvation Christ has brought to us, he could exult, 'Thanks be to God for his indescribable gift!' (2 Cor. 9:15). Hunger, pain, imprisonment, even the threat of death could not diminish this joy that sustained Paul in all his circumstances.

Whatever our present situation, however hard our circumstances, the cross of Christ promises us eternal peace and joy because of the goodness and kindness of God. The only legitimate response to this goodness is to worship our good God. We should desire to worship him. Paul admonishes us: 'Devote yourselves to prayer, being watchful and thankful' (Col. 4:2). A proper understanding of how good God is will not lead us to rush into his presence demanding blessings. Instead, 'In everything, by prayer and petition, with thanksgiving, present your requests to God' (Phil. 4:6). Thanksgiving is not a holiday in heaven, it is at the very center of unceasing worship of God (Rev. 4:9; 7:11-12), and so should also be the theme of our worship here on earth. We are to give thanks to God for his goodness.

Painful experiences in this life are actually to be seen as further evidence of God's goodness as he prepares us for glory. When we give thanks, we must not only do so for the nice and pleasant things we experience. We are to thank God for the unpleasant things that are used to teach us humility and holiness, and are necessary to draw us closer to him in dependence and faith. We give 'thanks to God the Father for everything, in the name of our Lord Jesus Christ' (Eph. 5:20; 1 Thess. 5:18). This is how thanking God becomes more than merely a mindless habit; it becomes an acknowledgment of him as the source of all good things and of our complete dependence on him. It is also a public testimony of a thankful life before a thankless world. Our generous and thankful giving to the work of the Church, whatever our financial circumstances, is both a testimony of God's goodness to us and a reflection of our desire to share this goodness with others who might not be aware of the one source of all goodness.

As the psalmist instructs us: 'Give thanks to the LORD, for he is good; his love endures forever' (Psalm 107:1)

Questions

1. What does the term 'goodness' mean?
2. Is God still good if he does not give us good things?
3. Relate some of the evidence that God is good to mankind.
4. Relate some of the evidence that God is good to you.
5. If God is good, how do you explain the pain and suffering in the world?
6. What is the relationship between God's goodness and Jesus' death on the cross?
7. How is goodness different from morality?
8. Can people be truly good in God's eyes?
9. Do you think that God values highly human thankfulness?
10. What motivates you to live a good life – a life that is kind, compassionate, patient, honest, thankful, loving, faithful?

Chapter Ten

Settled Hostility

The attribute of
Wrath

The wrath of God is being revealed from heaven against
all the godlessness and wickedness of men who suppress
the truth by their wickedness (Rom. 1:18)

In Deuteronomy, we find a most unusual concert. Moses, the man who has led the children of Israel for 40 years, is addressing the people one last time. He knows he is not to enter the promised land, and that God has told him the time is come for his death. What does Moses do? He sings, and in this song he describes the coming judgement of God on Israel.

> A fire has been kindled by my wrath, one that burns to the realm of death below. It will devour the earth and its harvests and set on fire the foundations of the mountains. I will heap calamities upon them and expend my arrows against them. I will send wasting famine against them, consuming pestilence and deadly plague... (Deut. 32:22-24).

Now, this obviously is not the sort of pep talk we would expect the leader to give his people before they begin the daunting task of inhabiting a new land. We would want encouragement, lots of positive thinking and not a hint of any negativity. We would want to be told everything was going to be just fine.

God ordained that Israel would be punished for its rebellious sins. And any honest reading of Scripture makes it very clear that the righteous God who poured out wrath on his stiff-necked people centuries ago is just as righteous today, just as offended by sin and rebellion against his sovereignty. It is a very uncomfortable truth, even to many Christians, who reject this 'outdated' concept of God. They apologize for such verses as these in Deuteronomy, and refuse to accept God's wrath as part of his character. Only sour old pessimists such as John Calvin could believe in a God of wrath! We want a gentle Jesus, meek and mild.

But the Bible does not hide the truth, nor apologize for the character of God. In fact, the Bible refers to the wrath of God as many times as it does to the love of God. Over 600 passages speak clearly of God's wrath, and Jesus Christ spoke of hell more often than anyone in Scripture. The meaning is clear: the holy God is a God of wrath to the unholy.

What is God's Wrath?

Wrath basically means anger. We humans understand anger very well, as it is on display almost every day, everywhere. But human anger is often selfish, vindictive, arbitrary, spiteful. Because our nature is flawed by sin, our anger manifests itself through the loss of temper and self-control. This is absolutely nothing like the righteous anger of God.

God's wrath is pure and holy, settled and permanent. It is a consistent attitude of hostility to all evil. We can know God's anger towards sin is righteous because it is rooted in his essential holiness. Any and all sin is, literally, a personal affront to God. Thus his wrath is his eternal, consistent opposition to sin and evil.

God is good. The devil and evil are hostile to God and all that is good. God cannot tolerate evil, he hates it. Christians who do not understand how great an affront sin is to God cannot accept the idea that God 'hates' anything or anyone. They want the kindly grandfather, not the righteous judge. But the justice of God demands punishment for evil, and his wrath guarantees it.

We must understand that God is not controlled by circumstances or emotions, and neither is his anger. It is an unyielding, permanent characteristic. The actions that his anger leads to are not spiteful; his vengeance is that of the judge. 'God is a righteous judge, a God who expresses his wrath every day' (Psalm 7:11).

How is God's wrath revealed today? It might surprise you to know that God actually punishes many people by allowing them to continue in the very sins that offend his righteousness. Their own evil becomes part of their judgment! 'God gave them over to the sinful desires of their hearts, to sexual impurity ... to shameful lusts ... to a depraved mind' (Rom. 1:24, 26, 28). We can see the results of this type of punishment all around us, in sexually transmitted diseases, in violent crime, in drug addiction, and in the general breakdown of Western society and its values. Our culture is reaping ten-fold what it spent decades sowing. This truly is evidence of the wrath of God. He is not passive or indifferent to sin, he actively opposes evil and will punish it.

Objections to God's Wrath

As mentioned earlier, the wrath of God is often misunderstood and equated with human anger. This is the basis for one common objection to the Biblical teaching of divine wrath. 'You thought I was like you,' says God (Psalm 50:21), but God is not like us, and his anger is very different from ours.

> What if God, choosing to show his wrath and make his power known, bore with great patience the objects of his wrath – prepared for destruction? What if he did this to make the riches of his glory known to the objects of his mercy, whom he prepared in advance for glory...? (Rom. 9:20-25).

God's wrath is patient, tempered by his mercy.

We must also recognize that people do not feel the full force of God's wrath here and now. That lies in the future. No matter how severe the present punishments might seem, they are only a foretaste of what awaits the unbeliever who rejects salvation. God gives a dire warning to unbelievers when he says: 'Because of your stubbornness and your unrepentant heart, you are storing up wrath against yourself for the day of God's wrath, when his righteous judgment will be revealed' (Rom. 2:5). It is only his great patience and kindness that restrains the full, righteous wrath of God in this present age.

There is a second common objection to the teaching of God's wrath. It is a moral one, the protest that such wrath is not fair, is not worthy of a loving, merciful God. Surely people do not deserve God's wrath – we may not be perfect, but we're not evil. Besides, it isn't our fault anyway. We really mean well, we just can't help ourselves. Surely a great God understands and will overlook our weaknesses, won't he?

The biblical answer is direct, and blunt: we are God's enemies. Sin puts us in direct opposition to the will and holiness of God. We aren't just disappointments to our kindly Creator, we are active rebels against the holy, sovereign God. And we are told clearly: 'The LORD takes vengeance on his foes and maintains his wrath against his enemies' (Nahum 1:2). By nature we are children of disobedience, and Romans 4:15 says transgression brings wrath.

God directs his wrath against 'the godlessness and wickedness of men who suppress the truth by their wickedness' (Rom. 1:18). We suppress and deny truth, especially the truth of our own deep-down sin and the truth of God's real character. We crave a God who is tolerant of evil, especially our evil. But God is a God of wrath. Jesus said: 'I will show you whom you should fear: fear him who, after the killing of the body, has the power to throw you into hell. Yes, I tell you, fear him' (Luke 12:5).

Yet God's wrath does not arise from feelings. He is a God

of wrath because he is a God of holiness, a God of justice. We deserve his wrath because of our rebellion and sin against his holy nature and his holy law.

Reasons for God's Wrath

The rebellion of the creatures against their Creator precipitated the first human experience with the wrath of God. When Adam and Eve sinned against God in the Garden of Eden, God immediately pronounced a curse on all mankind. Divine anger expelled Adam and Eve from the garden; ever since humankind has been alienated from God. We are strangers from his presence. God promised that the soul that sins shall die eternally. The sovereign, holy Lord of the universe will not be mocked or defied.

Mankind's daily disobedience of the law of God also arouses his anger. We do not lack for warnings of the penalty of sin, whether provided by Old Testament prophets or New Testament apostles: 'Let no one deceive you with empty words, for because of such things God's wrath comes on those who are disobedient' (Eph. 5:6).

The inhabitants of Sodom and Gomorrah experienced God's wrath, as did the people of Noah's time. The great flood in fact demonstrated God's wrath as well as symbolized the wrath of the Day of Judgement for all mankind which is yet to come. These two spectacular examples warn us of the penalty we incur from breaking God's laws. You see, breaking God's law is defiance of God personally, because the law reflects the heart of God. That is why sin is such a deadly, serious business.

The inhumanity of man to man takes many forms – injustice, cruelty, oppression, unfaithfulness. We value our judicial systems whereby a vandal or a rapist, a thief or a murderer receives just punishment for their offense against our codes of law. So if we expect justice from human judges, how much more should we expect justice from God when we violate his laws? Why should we be surprised to receive justice from God as expressed in his wrath at our sin? It is true that in our society the wicked appear often to escape any consequence of their evil, but that is a delusion. God is only delaying his wrath. A criminal may escape arrest and justice; the wicked will not escape God. True justice will one day be done, for unlike our courts and judges the justice of God is absolute and certain. 'God will give to each person according to what he has done' (Rom. 2:6-8).

Old Testament prophecy is full of such promises of judgment and justice. It is also evident in the New Testament, such as when Paul refers to the state as 'God's servant, an agent of wrath to bring punishment to the wrongdoer' (Rom. 13:4). We know that God uses the civil process to provide a temporary and imperfect wrath on evildoers. This is just a shadow of the divine wrath to come.

Too often in recent years Americans have watched their televisions in horrified fascination at the evidences of human wrath – violent, hateful anger directed at good and bad alike. The riots in Los Angeles following the trial of policemen who beat motorist Rodney King showed the nation what wrath can be: people running wild in the streets, looting shops, overturning cars, burning businesses, and attacking anyone they came across regardless of color. Violence, fire, destruction on the streets of one of the world's great cities, all for little reason. The fundamental reason had little to do with injustice or economics. This was the spiteful human rage that erupts from time to time unless checked by the common grace of God.

Compare this with the proceedings of the Nuremberg Trials following World War II. There in the tense but controlled atmosphere of a court, judges and juries heard testimony of the most horrific of human crimes. Evidence was presented and evaluated according to the rules agreed upon. Counsel for and against were listened to. Finally, in an air of calm deliberation, judgement was pronounced, sentence given, and the guilty were punished. Justice was done. This is how God expresses his wrath – not in the hateful screams of wild rioters or a lynch-mob, but in the sober, calm pronouncements of a just and holy court, enforcing established and righteous rules.

Above all, rejection of his Son arouses the wrath of God. The psalmist foretold opposition to Christ, and the eventual punishment of those who defy him:

> The kings of the earth take their stand and the rulers gather together against the LORD and against his anointed one.... The One enthroned in heaven laughs; the LORD scoffs at them. Then he rebukes them in his anger and terrifies them in his wrath (Psalm 2:2, 4, 5).

Read again, that God laughs and scoffs at all who attempt to oppose his will. Sin will result in wrath, but does not hinder God's purposes.

In fact, the evil deeds of mankind will serve God. This truth is best represented by the cross. There man directed his human wrath against Christ, but Christ achieved his victory in the Resurrection and returned to glory. He will return again to this earth to shower the wrath of God against those who have rejected his love, his patience, his kindness, and who have despised the shed blood of the Son of God.

How much more severely do you think a man deserves to be punished who has trampled the Son of God underfoot.... It is a dreadful thing to fall into the hands of the living God (Heb. 10:29, 31).

The book of Revelation paints terrible, vivid pictures of that great day of God's holy wrath, with warnings to flee from the wrath of the Lamb of God, Jesus Christ. How can we flee this judgment, this wrath? Flee to the cross and its offer of forgiveness, before it is too late. This is the *only* means of escaping the wrath of God. There is no attorney, no loophole, no appeal that can spare the condemned sinner from the terrible punishment that awaits those who despise the Lamb of God and his wonderful love. But there is no condemnation to those who are in Christ Jesus!

It is impossible to escape awareness of the wrath of God, since it is the subject of divine revelation from the third chapter of Genesis to the end of the book of Revelation. There is a purpose to this constant presentation of a God of wrath in Scripture. We cannot truly appreciate the love of God, until we appreciate his justice; and we cannot appreciate his justice until we appreciate his holiness. It is a holiness that demands justice, and justice brings wrath. Because our God is holy, just, and sovereign, he is a God of wrath. Thus, how great is his love in the light of his wrath.

This constant theme of justice and wrath is necessary, but when we consider it our hearts can fall victim to fear and depression. There is encouragement, however, in the source of salvation: the cross.

In the Garden of Gethsemane, our Savior pleaded with his Father to take away the horror of the cross (Mark 14:33-36). The Son of God was overwhelmed with fear, grief, horror, as he understood what the cross would mean for him. Read the words of Matthew closely, and the image is inescapable: 'Darkness came over all the land.... Jesus cried out in a loud voice... "My God, My God, why have you forsaken me?"'(Matt. 27:45-46). Darkness, pain, separation – the same fundamental fears of sinful man are found at the cross. This was where the wrath of God against human sin was poured out on to Jesus, where a holy God's fury was directed against his beloved Son. Justice was done, in a manner beyond our imagining.

When we look at the cross, we see the absolute seriousness of sin. We see, too, our hopeless, dreadful, just fate if not for the grace and love of God. Christ our Lord endured in our place the terrible hatred of God against sin and evil.

This is why we must know of the wrath of God in order to comprehend the immeasurable love of God. You see, Jesus experienced both, and thanks to his sacrifice we who are God's children have no fear of his wrath. The cup has been poured out and is empty of wrath to believers. Because of Jesus, we can experience his love. There truly is no more condemnation to us who are in Christ Jesus.

Conclusion

Since Christ appeased God's wrath against us (1 John 2:2; Rom. 3:24, 25), we should live lives of constant, humble gratitude. What if Jesus had not taken our place and suffered the wrath of God for us? What if Jesus had never invited us to come to him in simple faith? What if God were to treat us as we really deserve?

How thankful we should be that salvation is free! We are essentially no different from those who have been passed over and must appear before God at the day of wrath alone, without Christ as their advocate. We too were objects of wrath once, but are now objects of mercy by grace alone.

But we should be more than thankful, we should be worshipful. Our attitude as believers ought to be one of constant reverential awe and devotion, resulting in grateful and joyful public and private worship in daily lives. We are now to live for his glory, dedicated to the spread of God's gracious kingdom on earth and service to the body of Christ, the church.

Appreciating the terrible reality of God's wrath and the wonder of our own deliverance does not make us judges of unbelievers. To the contrary, it should give us compassionate hearts for those who are under condemnation. How great was our Savior's compassion! Perhaps the most heart-stopping words in the New Testament are 'Jesus wept'. Think of it. Jesus wept not only over the death of his close friend Lazarus and the sorrow of friends and family, but also over the future of Jerusalem. Look around you at your neighbors, your friends, those you work alongside. Can you see the cloud over their heads?

Consider the compassion of Moses, when he spoke with God on the mountaintop after the children of Israel had defied their Lord with idol worship. Moses knew the sin of the people, and God even proposed to make a new people from Moses. Yet the leader begged from a heart of compassion for the 'stiff-necked people' for mercy from a holy God. 'Oh, what a great sin these people have committed! They have made themselves gods of gold. But now, please forgive their sin – but if not, blot me out of the book you have written' (Exod. 32:31, 32).

Of course Moses could not die in the place of other sinners, for he, too, was sinful. But he was willing to. So was the apostle Paul, who was willing to be condemned if by this many could be forgiven (Rom. 9:3). How shallow is our compassion when compared to theirs!

The threat of God's wrath is always the lesser motive for evangelism; the glory of God and the love of Jesus should be the greatest motivation. It is the wrath of God that reminds us that all of life is real, important, brief, and completely dependent on God's grace.

Questions

1. What does the wrath of God mean?
2. If God were not a God of wrath, would his character be complete or deficient?
3. What does God hate, and why?
4. Is God right to be angry with mankind as it is today?
5. Are the wrath of God and the love of God contradictory ideas?
6. Why is it important for us to believe in the wrath of God?
7. Why is God especially angry when people reject the gospel?
8. How does the book of Revelation describe the 'day of God's wrath'?
9. Is God angry with you? Why, or why not?
10. How does the wrath of God motivate you?

Chapter Eleven

Perfect Love

The question of Love

Whoever does not love does not know God, for God is love
(1 John 4:8).

No more heartwarming statement exists in all the world's literature than this: God is love. Certainly Christians can take great comfort in this truth, which is one of three great statements God has given us in the Bible about his nature: God is Spirit, God is light, and God is love. Of these definitions the third is by far the most popular. Even people who have never read the Bible, or care nothing for God or his Son, enjoy hearing that he is love. These three precious words are so easy to say, and so very difficult to appreciate.

But what is this love that God is? In our culture, stating that 'God is love' suggests that he is an amiable, tolerant being, perhaps a bit weak, basically harmless and unthreatening. Nice, in other words. Sort of a year-round Santa Claus.

Love in English can mean anything from romance to lust, or any shading in between. Philosophers and poets alike have filled libraries pondering what love is, not that all their ideas are positive. 'Love is an ocean of emotions, surrounded by expenses,' stated Lord Dewar. 'Love is a conflict between reflexes and reflections,' said another cynic. And Plato was of the opinion that 'love is a grave mental disease'... and he didn't even have the advantage of our movies and novels! Swedenborg believed 'love is spiritual fire'.

The ancient Greeks clarified what they meant when they spoke or wrote of love, using four different words: (1) *eros*, or sexual love; (2) *philos*, for friendship; (3) *storge*, for affection, e.g., for pets; and (4) *agape*, for the giving of one's self to others. In Greek usage these are not completely separate and distinct ideas. Each word has a range of meaning, and sometimes one term can be substituted for another. Nevertheless the four terms point to differing emphases, or aspects of love, which we do well to appreciate.

When we are told God is love, what is meant is that God is *agape* love. He gives freely of his self to his creation, because *agape* love is his character. This giving love of God is a central theme of the Old Testament, where he gives life and direction to his creation. The New Testament then takes the gracious covenant-keeping love of God in the Old Testament, and fills it full of Jesus, God's gift of himself to us.

The Bible tells us a number of things about God's love.

Love is God's Nature

When John wrote *God is love* (1 John 4:8), he did not say God has love or God can love. He said God *is* love. Do you see the difference? Love is essential to God's being; he cannot be God without loving. This love does not require effort, it is the very core of his being. The hatred of sin that God shows is a reaction to what opposes him, but his love is what he is. The awesome truth is that God would be love even if there was *nothing* to love. No wonder Augustine quoted this verse 58 times in his writings!

Maximilian Kolbe, a Polish priest, was 45 years of age when the Nazis invaded Poland in September of 1939. Within a matter of weeks he and the other friars of Niepokalanow were arrested and taken to prison camp, only to be released a few weeks later. Kolbe at once went back to ministering to the sick and the fearful. He knew of Hitler's memo to the German occupation forces: 'They will preach what we want them to preach. If any priest acts differently, we will make short work of him. The task of the priest is to keep the Poles quiet, stupid, and dull-witted.'

On February 17, 1941, at 9 a.m., Father Kolbe was again arrested and this time sentenced to Auschwitz for publishing unapproved materials. When he arrived at the concentration camp in May he was informed that the average life expectancy of the clergy was about one month. Working on the timber detail and given meager rations, Kolbe soon collapsed. The guards beat and kicked him, dealt him fifty lashes and tossed his body in a ditch. Rescued by some other prisoners, Kolbe clung to life until July, when suddenly one night the camp was turned upside down by news that a prisoner had escaped. In retaliation, camp commandant Fritsch ordered that ten men be executed for the one escaped prisoner. Among those selected was a man called Palitsch, who cried out, 'My poor wife! My poor children! What will they do?'

Father Kolbe suddenly stepped before the guards, asking quietly, 'I would like to die in place of one of the men you condemned.' The commandant snapped, 'Why?' Diplomatically, Kolbe responded, 'I am an old man, sir, and good for nothing. My life will serve no purpose.' The ploy worked, and after identifying Palitsch as the man he would replace, Kolbe was led off to a windowless cell in Barracks 11, where he and the other nine men were left, naked, to die. On August 14, 1941, the last four men, including Father Kolbe, were killed by a lethal injection to make room for the next batch of condemned prisoners.

> Very rarely will anyone die for a righteous man, though for a good man, someone might possibly dare to die. But God demonstrated his own love for us in this: While we were still sinners, Christ died for us (Rom. 5:7, 8)

Love is God's Character

We can see the character of God in Jesus and in the Father's love for the Son. 'The reason my Father loves me is that I lay down my life – only to take it up again' (John 10:17). 'The

Father loves the Son and has placed everything in his hands' (John 3:35). The Father's love for the Son is the model of his love for us who are his children, made in his image.

1 Corinthians 13 describes the real character of God as well as the ideal character of the Christian. Substituting 'God' for 'love', verses 4-8 now read: 'God is patient, God is kind. God does not envy, God does not boast, God is not proud. God is not rude, God is not self-seeking, God is not easily angered, God keeps no record of wrongs. God does not delight in evil but rejoices with the truth. God always protects, always trusts, always perseveres. God never fails.' God's character is totally loving in all these ways. He is not ruled by some law above himself; he is ruled by love within himself.

Love is Sovereign

Because God is sovereign and free, he is able to love whomever he chooses, even sinners opposed to him and his will. He told Israel: 'The LORD did not set his affection on you and choose you because you were more numerous than other peoples, for you were the fewest of all peoples. But it was because the Lord loved you...' (Deut. 7:7-8). There is no cause in us – certainly not our love for him – that would incite his love for us. As John said, 'We love him because he first loved us.'

If you have been delivered from the kingdom of darkness to the kingdom of light, from wrath to salvation, you surely have asked yourself at some point, 'Why me? Why was I chosen and not others?' How God chooses those who are his is one of the mysteries he has not revealed to us. Just the fact of his undeserved love for us is so amazing, so incomprehensible, that we may say with Isaac Watts:

Were the whole realm of nature mine,
that were a present far too small;
love so amazing, so divine,
demands my soul, my life, my all.

In Romans 9:13, Paul cited the Old Testament passage, 'Jacob have I loved, Esau have I hated.' Yes, God loves all of his creation, but his *saving* love is particular and specific. God is not egalitarian. Paul, under the guidance of the Holy Spirit, addressed the Colossian church as 'God's chosen people and dearly loved'. God's love for his people is intimate and passionate, because it is directed to those whom he personally selected. In the very first family, God chose to honor the offering of Abel, not Cain, and still today his love is specific: 'We always ought to thank God for you brothers loved by the Lord, because from the beginning God chose you to be saved through the sanctifying work of the Spirit and through belief in the truth' (2 Thess. 2:13).

Some people are not comfortable with the doctrines of election and predestination, but these doctrines are the fruit of God's wonderful, sovereign love:

Praise be to the God and Father of our Lord Jesus Christ... for he chose us in him before the creation of the world to be holy and blameless in his sight. In love he predestined us to be adopted as his Sons through Jesus Christ, in accordance with his pleasure and will – to the praise of his glorious grace (Eph. 1:3-5).

Behind the doctrine of predestination lies the sovereign love of God. His choice is a loving choice, although it is shrouded in mystery to us.

I carried my six-month-old daughter to the top of the stairs and began to descend. As I did so, I held her above my head and gazed with adoration into the eyes of this beautiful bundle of joy and murmured loving nonsense to her. I don't know why, but she suddenly jerked around in my hands, and I lost my grip on her. From the top of the stairs I saw with sudden horror the little body fly into the air. My reaction was immediate: I dived forward down the flight of stairs, caught my daughter in mid-air, twisted my body and landed underneath her at the foot of the stairs. My back was injured, but through the pain I thanked God that my baby was safe and unhurt. If I had calmly considered what to do before I did it, I might not have done it, or not acted in time. But as the great French philosopher, Blaise Pascal, put it: 'The heart has reasons, reason has no knowledge of.'

Love Is Everlasting

> The LORD appeared to us in the past, saying, 'I have loved you with an everlasting love; I have drawn you with kindness. I will build you up again and you will be rebuilt, O Virgin Israel. Again you will take up your tambourines and go out to dance with the joyful' (Jer. 31:3-4).

The love of God originates in eternity, and nothing in time and space can cause the Lord to change his love. We can count on his love.

The Song of Solomon says that 'Love is as strong as death'. The apostle Paul goes further in that glorious, reassuring passage in Romans 8:38-39:

> I am convinced that neither death nor life, neither angels nor demons, neither the present nor the future, nor any powers, neither height nor depth, nor anything else in all creation, will be able to separate us from the love of God that is in Christ Jesus our Lord.

The love of God is unquenchable – the entire universe of evil cannot cool it in the least. What joy and confidence should be ours as we meditate on his everlasting love!

Love Is Powerful

Do you realize that love is powerful? We have already seen what Paul says about the power of God's love in Romans 8, that nothing can come between God and one he loves. Paul's prayer for the Ephesians was that they would have 'power, together with all the saints, to grasp how wide and long and high and deep is the love of Christ, and to know this love that surpasses knowledge' (Eph. 3:18-19). Why power? Because the love of God is so great and so mighty that it will take our entire lifetimes to begin to appreciate it even a little. His love is infinite and immeasurable and effective, so much so that it overcomes the barriers of sin and God's own wrath and judgment. It even overcomes death. The resurrection of Jesus guarantees the victory of God's love forever.

John 3:16 speaks about the measure and power of God's love – a love so great that the holy God can love even this corrupt, sinful world in all its ugliness, shame, and rebellion. It is a love so great that he sacrificed his own beloved Son to rescue this world.

Man under the law is surrounded by the wrath of God. But man in Christ is surrounded by the all-powerful love of God. No wonder John exclaimed: 'How great is his love that he has lavished on us, that we should be called the children of God!' (1 John 3:1). This love for the church is also portrayed in the Old Testament books of Ezekiel and Hosea, as the forgiving love of a husband for an adulterous wife. He takes believers back and forgives again and again because he loves the church with a love that cannot be stopped.

Love Is Active

Lieutenant McCrary and two of his men were caught behind the enemy lines in Vietnam. They had been sent on a reconnaissance patrol of a wooded hill, and unknown to them the Vietcong had moved forward at the same time. Now the Americans were surrounded, cut off from their base. At once they called for a helicopter to evacuate them and settled in to await rescue. But shortly before the chopper arrived, the Vietcong spotted their position and began to move in.

Suddenly a grenade landed in front of all three soldiers. Before McCrary could react, one of his men leaped onto the grenade just before it exploded, thus saving the lives of his comrades. Without a second thought this man gave his life for his friends.

God's *agape* love is self-giving love. It is active, not passive. God actively gave of himself to us in and through his Son Jesus. As John 3:16 reminds us, God so loved the world that he gave his only Beloved Son. Or as Paul said in Ephesians 5:25: 'Christ loved the church and gave himself for her.' John defined love in active terms also: 'This is how we know what love is: Jesus Christ laid down his life for us' (1 John 3:16). God demonstrated his great, active love in all its depth and extent by sending his Son to die for us and raise us up to live in the presence of his eternal love forever. 'This is love: not that we loved God, but that he loved us and sent his Son as an atoning sacrifice for our sins' (1 John 4:10).

God's active love motivates us to love him and to love others. 'Live a life of love...' (Eph. 5:2). God's love continues to be active in our lives as he daily cares for us and assures us of our eternal salvation. Every morning when we awake, we may joyfully assert: 'I have been crucified with

Christ and I no longer live, but Christ lives in me. The life I live in the body I live by faith in the Son of God who loved me and gave himself for me' (Gal. 2:20).

Love Is Revealed by Jesus

'The Father loves the Son and has placed everything in his hands' (John 3:35). Jesus showed us the love of God in actions we can understand – in his meek and caring attitude, in his miracles of healing, in his acts of forgiveness, in his gracious teaching, and especially in his self-sacrificing death. This is the love of God expressed in visible, tangible terms. It is love we can safely put our trust in, as surely as the Father has placed everything in the hands of Christ.

You see, our God is not a God who philosophizes about love or who merely sends us pleasant letters from a far distance about his lovely feelings for us. No, he came to us in love, showing his heart in the life and actions of Jesus even at the terrible cost of the cross.

Love Is Focused on the Cross

The depth of God's love was pictured centuries before the actual events that culminated in the cross. Isaiah was given an amazing prophecy in chapter 53 of the Lamb of God being led to the slaughter to be cruelly put to death.

God asked Abraham to sacrifice his son Isaac, then he mercifully provided a substitute and thus spared this trusting father a horrible, agonizing act. But God the Father did not spare his own Son. Instead of halting Jesus' agony at the last instant, the Father gave up his Son for our redemption. And the Son gave himself up as well. 'No greater love has a man than this,' Christ said, 'than that he give his life for his friends.' He gave his life for us on the cross, suffering hell for us. There truly is no greater love.

Love Is Purposeful

The cross of Christ does not make God love us. On the contrary, God's love for us provided us with the cross and salvation. God has a purpose in loving us: to redeem us, and to enable us to spend eternity loving and worshiping him who loved us first. Read Romans 8:28-39. The love of God wills and accomplishes the fruits of his saving purposes for humanity, and his sovereign power guarantees the fruits of his love. Suffering and discipline are but part of his final, loving purpose to make us like Jesus Christ his Son.

Love Is Experiential

Most Christians are embarrassed about our own lack of love for God. We should be! Our love for God is a by-product of knowing experientially his love for us. That is, we tend to love God only as much as we feel we are loved by him. Naturally we seldom begin to appreciate the breadth, depth, and height of his love.

You cannot know what strawberries taste like by seeing pictures, learning their chemical composition, and comparing them to other fruits. Until you taste a strawberry, you cannot have certain knowledge of strawberries. The psalmist has said: 'Taste and see that God is good' (Psalm 34:8).

Paul asserted in Romans 5:5: 'God has poured out his love into our hearts by the Holy Spirit, whom he has given us.' This flood of God's love comes to us at conversion, but to maintain the flow we must come often to drink at the fountain of his love. Jesus invites us to quench our soul's thirst by coming to him in faith. We do that by reading his words, calling to him in prayer and worship, and obeying the command to share his love with others. And as John tells us,

'Perfect love casts out fear' (1 John 4:18). Our experience of his love drives away the experiences of fears and doubts.

Conclusion

'Dear friends, let us love one another, for love comes from God. Whoever does not love does not know God, for God is love' (1 John 4:7, 8). This is the simple biblical conclusion to what we know about God's loving nature. But you may realize that your nature is not so loving. You may even be ashamed at your lack of love for people, and even for the Lord himself. Quite right! So am I.

But remember, biblical love is not a matter of feelings. It is a choice, a matter of the will. Love is a decision to do what is good and kind and generous to others, despite whatever we feel inside. It is a commitment that has to be renewed every day to honor and serve and worship the Lord.

The Heidelberg Catechism defines the Christian life as a life lived out of gratitude. If we are truly grateful for the love God has shown to us, we will want to love God back and love our neighbor as ourselves. If that is not happening, we need to spend more prayerful time meditating on the truths of God's love as revealed in Scripture, and then find someone to love sacrificially regardless of our inner doubts and fears. And believe it or not, the right feelings will follow our obedience of love.

Does God's love move you to do anything? And what will you do for God this week, just out of love?

Questions

1. What is love, according to the Bible?
2. What is our modern, Hollywood concept of love?
3. Relate the four Greek words for love and their usual meanings.
4. Explain how God loves all mankind but saves only some for eternal life.
5. How does the book of Hosea portray the love of God for the church?
6. Does God love us because he elected us, or does God elect us because he loves us, or both?
7. Does God's love for you change for any reason?
8. What is the supreme proof of God's love?
9. What is the importance of 1 Corinthians 13?
10. What is the solution to our lack of appreciation for God's love to us?

1. What is love according to the Bible?

2. Where can human love and God's love be...

3. Is it true that those who love are forgiven and that love...

4. Explain how God loves all mankind but even more particular in...

5. Is love the best of all the gospel message?...

6. Does ... to love us because we ... disobey our or God's commands...

7. Does God love us too ... for us even though we...

8. What is the importance of ... compassion and...

9. In what way is love to ... and... to simplicity love ...

Chapter Twelve

Total Consistency

The attribute of
Faithfulness

*Because of the LORD's great love we are not consumed,
for his compassions never fail. They are new every
morning; great is your faithfulness* (Lam. 3:22, 23).

These verses from Lamentations 3 are reflected in one of the church's favorite hymns, 'Great is Thy Faithfulness'. The hard-earned experience of God's people in their exile in Babylon is the background of the passage. They looked at the sorry history of their own behavior and at the whole history of God's dealings with them. They realized that though they had changed and had failed to keep the covenant, God had not changed. He had been faithful to the covenant, and he remained faithful to his people. Though captured, enslaved, and far removed from the Promised Land, they were not consumed. God's compassions had not failed.

Faithfulness is one of the most important characteristics that we must appreciate in our Lord. When life does not make sense, or when our feelings drown the faith in our hearts, our knowledge of God's faithfulness will help sustain us.

Darren told me recently of an elderly lady he knows in his church who is an inspiration to him. As a young woman Anna traveled with her husband and three children to Africa, where they worked in evangelism and church-planting. After a period of rapid growth for the church and the Bible school, members began attending more liberal, trendy churches. Within a few years the attendance at both their church and Bible school dwindled to almost nothing. About this time their youngest son was killed in a motorbike accident. Shortly after the family returned to the United States the oldest son turned away from the faith. He still shows no interest in the gospel of God's love.

Although this is not an evangelical success story, it is an example of patient faithfulness shown by Anna. She does not grumble against God's providence, nor does she show self-pity at the losses their family has suffered. This mother prays for her son constantly, then gets on with her life of serving others in the church, trusting confidently in the wisdom and goodness of the long-term purposes of God. Darren tells me her faithfulness is his inspiration whenever he becomes discouraged, and is an evident proof of the faithfulness of the God who sustains her.

Faithfulness in the Bible means trustworthiness, reliability, constancy, credibility. The living God is dependable – we can count on him. He will never fail or falter or let us down. This is why his word can be believed, and his actions will always be consistent with his words. The faithful God holds true to his promises, whether made to a nation in captivity or a mother grieving over a strayed son. He will do what he says, always.

Rudyard Kipling in his poem 'The Thousandth Man' describes the value of true friendship:

> One man in a thousand, Solomon says,
> Will stick more close than a brother.
> And it's worth while seeking him half your days
> If you find him before the other.
> Nine hundred and ninety-nine depend
> On what the world sees in you,
> But the Thousandth Man will stand your friend
> With the whole world round agin you.

The Old Testament portrays such true, beautiful friendship in the lives of David and Jonathan, of Ruth and Naomi, and many others. But the glory of the New Testament is that the friend who sticks closer than a brother, to all believers, is the Lord Jesus. He alone is totally and completely faithful to his friends.

God's Faithfulness Does Not Change

God is again different from humanity in his eternal faithfulness. We have seen in a previous chapter that in some ways God does change, and in other ways he will not change, but God's unchanging nature and character guarantee that he will remain faithful in all his relations with us.

In Malachi 3:6 God says, 'I, the LORD, do not change.' In the New Testament, Hebrews 13:8, we read that 'Jesus Christ is the same yesterday, today, and forever'. These passages refer to God's essential nature, as does 2 Timothy 2:13: 'If we are faithless, he will remain faithful, for he cannot disown himself.' Because God's nature is consistent and unchanging, he cannot contradict or compromise himself! This is how we can know that the God who is faithful to himself will be faithful to us. Faithfulness is his natural environment.

This is important to changeable, inconsistent creatures like ourselves who live in constantly shifting environments. In the midst of uncertainty we can have confidence in a faithful God. 'You are mighty, O LORD, and your faithfulness surrounds you' (Psalm 89:8).

God's Character

Even more important for us to understand is the eternal faithfulness of his character. Moses tells us in Deuteronomy 7, for example, that when God establishes his covenant with people he sticks to it. In Numbers we find the telling verse: 'God is not a man, that he should lie, nor a son of man, that he should change his mind. Does he speak and then not act? Does he promise and then not fulfill?' (Num 23:19). Such faithfulness is a rebuke to sinful humanity, which changes with the wind or on a whim. *God's moral character is consistent*. He is not a static idea or concept, but a sovereign Person who will always make the right moral choices. He has to, because it is his eternal nature and character.

God's faithfulness means he cannot fail or falter in his promises, or forget his word. Neither will he change the terms of his covenant. A word from God is more binding than a contract designed by a legion of lawyers: 'He is the rock, his words are perfect, and all his ways are just. A faithful God who does no wrong, upright and just is he' (Deut. 32:4). He promised after the great flood that the seasons of the year would always continue, and he has kept his word.

God's Purposes

Not only is God faithful in his nature and his character, but he is faithful in his purposes. Through the Old Testament prophet Isaiah, God promised the incarnation of his Son: 'The virgin shall be with child, and will call him Emmanuel' (Isa. 7:14). Centuries later, the apostle Paul could look at the prophecy fulfilled and record in Galatians 4:4: 'When the time had fully come, God sent his Son, born of a woman, born under law, to redeem those under law, that we might receive the full rights as sons.' An apparently impossible promise spoken hundreds of years before came to pass because God keeps his promises to accomplish his goal.

God upholds the planetary bodies because he is faithful and consistent in his purposes as well as in his nature and character. When Jesus Christ said he would defeat the devil, there were doubters. Yet he did, in a manner unimagined – but again foretold in the Old Testament. One of the great joys of Scripture study is reading the promises of God, then finding their fulfillment in time. The Bible is the history of

God's faithfulness! Of course, not all promises are encouraging. When the churches in Revelation 1-3 did not repent in spite of direct warnings from God, he did exactly as he said he would do.

The lesson is clearly that the promises of God can be counted on. They are consistent with his nature and character. 'The one who calls you is faithful and he will do it!' (1 Thess. 5:24).

Janine and Maurice were young and immature Christians, and wildly in love with each other. But lacking the biblical knowledge and faith to successfully deal with the natural temptations of a dating relationship, they made the same mistake so many other self-confident youngsters have made. At sixteen, Janine became pregnant. They realized at once, too late, that they had done wrong, but they were determined not to commit another wrong. So, they married and had their first child.

Janine later told me: 'When we got married, we immediately asked God to forgive our sin and to bless our union. It is amazing how he has answered that prayer! My husband went on to finish school and has a good job; I am almost through school, too. We have a wonderful son who has already asked Jesus into his heart, and God has even seen fit to use us in his service. When we asked God to forgive us, he was faithful. He has blessed our marriage. Don't be afraid to come back to God when you have failed! He will and does work all things together for good in the lives of those who love him and are called according to his purpose.'

So, God's faithfulness means that our Lord is just and cannot become unjust. He is loving and will never cease to be a loving God. He is omnipotent and cannot become weak. He has a perfect, complete character, and he cannot develop any characteristics that he does not already have. And he cannot become better or worse because he is perfect in his nature, character, and purposes.

But now let us look at the other side of this coin. We have seen the faithful God does not change in regard to his nature and character, nor in his purposes. But how does he change? Recall the earlier chapter called 'The Rock' and the examples of how the unchanging God changes in his relationships and his attitudes, as we react to him.

Attitude: God's holy nature remains the same, but his attitude is different towards different objects and people. He hates what is evil and loves what is holy. Thus, God's attitude of wrath to the sinner is changed to love for the forgiven sinner, as the judge becomes the Father.

Actions: As God's attitude toward us depends on our moral character, so does his actions. Remember the classic example of God's dealing with the Ninevites. When God sent Jonah with the warning of destruction, the people of the city repented and God's actions towards them changed. Jonah did not understand what God was doing, and thought he should go ahead and punish these heathens just as he had promised. But God said then, as he has said many other times, that he had repented, changed his mind, because the character of the people had changed.

Relationships: Finally, God changes in his relationship to individuals. In Ephesians 2:1-8 Paul teaches that God's relationship to us was once one of wrath and condemnation, which was demanded by his holiness and justice. His attitude towards us was changed when he gave us forgiveness and faith to believe in Jesus Christ as Lord and Savior. The result is a changed relationship: the child of wrath is a child of God, literally adopted into his own family with the gift of Christ's perfect righteousness. He loves us and always will love us because we are in Christ; we are righteous in his sight. And nothing can separate us from the love of God.

We can see that God can and will alter his mode of operation, changing the methods he was using to accomplish his purposes to suit the changed circumstances. In other words, his providence is variable, but his goals are not.

This helps us appreciate the relationship between the Old Testament and the New Testament. God's will never changes, because his character and knowledge are perfect. But God expresses his will in different ways in different periods of human time. A good example is the Old Testament command to sacrifice lambs as a sin-offering. It would be wrong for the Christian to obey this command today, because we are freed from the sacrificial system by Christ, the Lamb of God. Yet there is no contradiction here; it is a development of God's will from partial atonement to complete atonement, from provisional forgiveness to final forgiveness. The law of God continues forever, but the expression and application of that law changes and develops over time. The promises of God remain in force, but some are fulfilled and replaced by others.

Because of his unchanging nature, character and purposes, God is always and completely faithful, reliable and consistent. But his providence toward man and his relationship with man vary and alter *within the context* of his unchanging purposes. God is not static or unmoved. He is a living, feeling, thinking Creator who is sovereign and free to vary his methods and means while remaining always the same in his faithful character, nature, and purpose.

Faithfulness in Providence

God's faithfulness guarantees the provision of all our needs. In Matthew 6:25-34, the Lord Jesus compared our Father's faithfulness toward us with his continuous provision for the flowers and the birds he created. Since God is completely faithful toward, relatively speaking, unimportant creatures, providing the sustenance they need to survive, how could he possibly be less kind towards human beings made in his own image? Such a notion becomes ridiculous when you consider the infinite value the Father places on his children by sacrificing his own Son to redeem them from the guilt and power of sin. If the Lord is totally faithful in his dealing with even the more modest aspects of creation, we can be certain of his complete faithfulness to those whom he loved eternally and is now preparing a place for in heaven. Hence, Jesus tells us, it is foolish and sinful to worry about our needs. He will provide for them, because he is faithful to his Word.

God's faithfulness also guarantees our preservation. Do you ever worry that you might fall away from grace, or that you might be lost eternally? Listen to Paul in 1 Corinthians 1:8, 9:

> He will keep you strong to the end, so that you will be called blameless on the Day of our Lord Jesus Christ. God, who has called you into fellowship with his Son Jesus Christ our Lord, is faithful.

The work he began to do he will complete. God does not leave a job half-finished as we often do. The perseverance of all true believers unto death and beyond to glory is guaranteed, not by our efforts or sincerity, but by his faithfulness to those he loves. 'No one will pluck you out of my hand,' said our Savior (John 10:28). No experience in this life will prevent the Lord from preserving us for heaven, no matter how many ups and downs we have along the way. 'So, then, those who suffer according to God's will should commit themselves to their faithful Creator and continue to do good' (1 Pet. 4:19).

God's faithfulness guarantees our protection from real harm: 'The Lord is faithful, and he will strengthen and protect you from the evil one' (2 Thess. 3:3). The Christian need not (and should not) fear even the devil himself. Although we will surely experience many crises in our earthly lives, God is faithful in preserving us from real disaster. He brings us ultimately through every crisis, making us stronger and wiser for the battles ahead, until we are made perfect through suffering. King David discovered this and lived it out repeatedly!

The famous story in 1 Samuel 24 tells of Saul and his 3,000 men seeking David's life, pursuing and harrying him and eventually cornering him in a cave in the hills. Exhausted and frightened, David and his handful of men hid in the back of the cave. Suddenly Saul appeared at the mouth of the cave and entered without seeing David and his troops, and proceeded to relieve himself. David's men naturally urged their leader to take advantage of his enemy's helpless condition and kill him. After all, had not David been anointed to be King? Yet David refused, and instead crept up on Saul and sliced off a corner of the royal robe. When Saul had returned to the camp, David called out to him and showed the piece of robe, and told the king that he had spared his life out of respect for the office and the will of God.

Refusing to act in the place of God, David trusted God to deal with Saul in his own time, which indeed God did. David was able to behave like this because he understood and trusted in the utter faithfulness of God to fulfill his promise. Unlike many of us, David did not attempt to manipulate the will or actions of God. Thus he could write later that God was his protective shield.

God's faithfulness guarantees our deliverance from temptation, when we trust in him. Joseph's trust in God to deliver him was sorely tried in Egypt, when the handsome young Hebrew was tempted by the wife of his master Potiphar. Although Joseph would suffer years in jail as the result of rejecting this woman's advances, he continued to believe that his God was faithful. An even greater trial for Joseph was the temptation to hate his brothers for their betrayal and cruelty. Yet many years later, when these same treacherous men came to him as paupers, begging for grain, Joseph forgave them and eventually welcomed them into his own household, providing for them as God had provided for him.

An even greater example of trusting God in the face of temptation is that of our Savior, whose reaction to the tempting of Satan in the wilderness was to rely on the written promises of his Father. Notice, that the Son of God rebuked the tempter not in his own authority, but with Scripture. And finally, there was the ultimate temptation in the Garden of Gethsemane to say, 'Enough! I'll suffer no more for these people! I've done enough – not the cross, Father, not the cross!' But having faced the temptation to escape humiliation, suffering and death, Christ could say with a perfect faith: 'Nevertheless, not my will be done, Father, but yours.'

The Father is just as faithful in delivering us from temptations as he was to his own Son, provided only that we trust him as Jesus did:

> No temptation has seized you except what is common to man. And God is faithful; he will not let you be tempted beyond what you can bear. But when you are tempted, he will provide a way out so that you can bear up under it (1 Cor. 10:13).

Conclusion

That God is faithful helps us in prayer. The same, reliable God who has always blessed and preserved his people and answered their prayers is the One that we can come to in prayer today. He always has responded to the prayers of his people when they trusted him, and he always will. We can rest assured that the God we call upon to deliver us, to guide us, to perfect us, is the same God who guided Abraham across desert, mountain, and river to a land that he would give him. We come to the same God, who has not changed!

This is the great comfort to our fickle faith. You see, whether we trust him consistently or not, he remains trustworthy. We have learned that he is consistent and faithful, and when we read the history of his faithfulness we see how foolish it is not to have a perfect confidence in him in our times of crisis.

The faithfulness of God means that those who are made in his image are accountable for becoming more like him. That is why we have been given the Holy Spirit to renew us in God's image, which includes developing a character that will be faithful in our relationships as he is with us.

Finally, that God is faithful means we have a sure and certain hope for the future and that our worries are foolish. When Jesus Christ said 'Fear not, I will return and take you to be with Me,' we can know that he will. We can count on him. He will never leave nor forsake us. Just as millions of believers have found him to be totally faithful to his nature and his Word, you can rely on him, too. And this, you must agree, is truly awesome!

May God himself, the God of peace, sanctify you through and through. May your whole spirit, soul and body be kept blameless at the coming of our Lord Jesus Christ. The one who calls you is faithful and he will do it (1 Thess. 5:23,24).

Questions

1. What does it mean to say 'God is faithful'?
2. What does the biblical doctrine of the covenant contribute to our understanding of the faithfulness of God?
3. Relate examples of God's faithfulness to his people in the Old Testament.
4. Relate examples of God's faithfulness to you.
5. Jesus said, 'You are my friends.' What does this suggest to you?
6. What difference will the truth of God's faithfulness make to you when you are facing death?
7. Strong temptations can be very stressful. How can the doctrine of God's faithfulness help you to deal with them?
8. If a person habitually worries, does he or she really believe God is faithful?
9. Can humans be totally faithful?
10. What motivates you to be faithful in trusting God?

THE AUTHOR

Ken M. Campbell is an Associate Professor of Biblical Studies at Belhaven College, Jackson, Mississippi. Formerly a pastor of a Presbyterian church in upstate New York, he holds degrees from the University of Aberdeen (M.A.), Westminster Theological Seminary (B.D., Th.M.), and the University of Manchester (Ph.D.).